THE NEW ORTHODOXY

THE UNIVERSITY OF CHICAGO PRESS
CHICAGO, ILLINOIS

—

THE BAKER & TAYLOR COMPANY
NEW YORK

THE CAMBRIDGE UNIVERSITY PRESS
LONDON

THE MARUZEN-KABUSHIKI-KAISHA
TOKYO, OSAKA, KYOTO, FUKUOKA, SENDAI

THE MISSION BOOK COMPANY
SHANGHAI

THE
NEW ORTHODOXY

By
EDWARD SCRIBNER AMES

*Author of "The Psychology of Religious Experience," "The Higher
Individualism," and "The Divinity of Christ"*

THE UNIVERSITY OF CHICAGO PRESS
CHICAGO, ILLINOIS

Composed and Printed By
The University of Chicago Press
Chicago, Illinois, U.S.A.

PREFACE TO THE FIRST EDITION

At the present time many circumstances contribute to the demand for brief, constructive statements of religion. Technical scholarship in numerous fields has furnished rich and abundant materials, but they are not easy of access to the general reader. In the future these will be more adequately organized and vitalized in comprehensive interpretations. At the moment men's minds are impatient of elaboration and speculation. The war has developed inquiry concerning these questions with characteristic directness and poignancy. Already it has elicited remarkable activity in the restatement of traditional faiths. But no earnestness in the reaffirmation of the conventional views can satisfy those who are really awake to the problems and outlook of these days.

A new world of thought and ideals has arisen. Religion has its place in this new order, not as something aloof, but as something organic and integral with all other vital interests. All who truly dwell in this new world of the natural and the social sciences have certain attitudes and habits of thought in common. These constitute the new orthodoxy of method and spirit. It differs from the old orthodoxy as chemistry differs from alchemy and as empirical, reasonable beliefs differ from the dogmas of tradition imposed by external authority.

This book seeks to present in simple terms a view of religion consistent with the mental habits of those trained in the sciences, in the professions, and in the expert direction of practical affairs. It suggests a dynamic, dramatic conception designed to offer a means of getting behind specific forms and doctrines. It aims to afford a standpoint from which one may realize the process in which ceremonials and beliefs arise and through which they are modified. When thus seen religion discloses a deeper, more intimate, and more appealing character. As here conceived it is essentially the dramatic movement of the idealizing, outreaching life of man in the midst of his practical, social tasks. The problems of the religious sentiments, of personality, of sacred literature, of religious ideals, and of the ceremonials of worship are other terms which might have been employed as the titles of the successive chapters.

E. S. A.

PREFACE TO THE SECOND EDITION

A new edition of this book presents an opportunity for a further definition of orthodoxy, both of the old and the new. The orthodox view of religion may ordinarily be regarded as the prevailing view, but in a time like the present when even popular thought is being awakened by surprising discoveries and unprecedented methods of study and interpretation, a more discriminating use of terms is demanded. A lady to whom this book was recommended remarked upon observing its title, "No, thank you, I do not care to read anything that is orthodox." Her conception was doubtless much the same as that of a "liberal" minister who recently wrote: "All religions tend toward orthodoxy, that is toward changing from something vital and flowing to a static set of doctrines and a cramped attitude of mind." This he regards as apostasy from "the principle of free inquiry into all questions bearing upon the religious life."

It is the purpose of this book to insist that there has come into the world a new orthodoxy which is precisely the maintenance of this principle of free inquiry. Orthodoxy means right thinking. It does not properly signify adherence to a fixed system of dogmas, and certainly is not to be identified with a bigoted or prejudiced attitude of mind. It is true that in the past, religious thought, and also all other kinds of thought, sought too much for static, unchangeable truths. But that is no longer considered right thinking. Science in every field has shown the necessity and the advantage of the open mind. It does not endeavor merely to reproduce the past or to expound authoritative, traditional beliefs. It regards life as a forward-moving process, marked by discovery, novelty, and adventure. Consequently, the tables are completely turned. The old orthodoxy, in so far as it denounces free inquiry, questioning, and doubt, has become the great apostasy. It hinders experimentation and inhibits growth. The new orthodoxy is an attitude which welcomes investigation, seeks release from bondage to authority, and cherishes faith in the possibility of a fuller, richer life.

Yet the new recognizes a certain continuity with the old. Even though the old orthodoxy disclaims any kinship with the new, still the new insistently regards itself as a champion of the best things of an ancient developing faith springing from a deep soil and a hardy root in the spiritual nature of man. An important feature of the new orthodoxy is this appreciation of history and of the stages through which religion has become what it is today. This continuity is also psychological. Religion of all kinds moves primarily in the emotional and volitional levels of experience. Ideas, doctrines, and beliefs are projections from these profounder depths. They are very important and have much significance but they are not primary. They react upon the impulsive life, but they do not create it nor do they often succeed in displacing it.

Religion arises from real needs, from the need for companionship in great undertakings, for comfort in defeat and loss, for courage to go on with hard tasks, for pictures of future success after hard travail of soul. The stories of Old Testament heroes are stories of love, adventure, and patriotism, infused with a sense of divine purposes and angelic messengers. The story of the New Testament is a continuation of the old romance of faith with new characters and new scenery. Modern religion voices the same hunger and thirst for righteousness and justice and peace in a world of railways and electric lights. Men still listen eagerly for prophetic words, and long for escape from their mistakes and their sins. With the same wistful faces they strive to lift the veil from the mysteries about them. The fact that they have accumulated more experience and have devised more clever instruments in the quest does not quench their zest. The quest still continues.

Religion, like art and science, arises in human experience from the fact that man lives his life in a double fashion, in immediate experience and in imagination, and forever weaves the two together. He plows his fields in fact and also in ceremonial drama. He sings plaintively when lost or overthrown and shouts joyously when victorious. The hunter trails the beast of prey to death and draws pictures of the kill. All man's days are lived in the warmth of friendship and in fear of foes, and the life of his imagination is filled with mightier friends and deadlier foes. Struggling to realize his wishes in the little circle of his hearth and neighborhood, he feels the whole world carries patterns of his own moral warfare. A dynamic, outreaching urge, an expansive energy of will, is the basic fact. The intellectual forms in which it is embodied, and by which to some extent it is directed and controlled, are developments and elaborations. Man naturally loves his life and all that furthers and enlarges it. This will to live is the source of his values. In his reflective moments he seeks to understand and to assess them. In his appreciative moods he contemplates and enjoys them, is moved and inspired by them. Religion, in all ages, is devotion to these values, expressed in ceremonials, meditation, and good works. Just what the specific values are and the hierarchy in which they are placed depends upon the cultures of particular groups and the stages of their development. Likewise, the symbols of these values change, always bearing an intimate and vital relation to the general life in which they appear.

This maintenance and representation of values is the important thing. The old way of thinking is solicitous that the new way does not secure and cherish them, and is therefore distrustful of it. But the new orthodoxy is profoundly concerned with all the ideal values of life, and it is just because of this concern that it seeks to think about them in the way that is most clarifying and convincing. It holds that the values which constitute the soul of religion—love of life, reverence for its concrete forms, appreciation for great perspectives both toward the past and the future, trust in its growing ideals—enter into many types of symbolism, liturgical and creedal, and that they will continue to do so.   Religion thus conceived keeps its hold upon the actual realities of man's normal existence but at the same time lifts the imagination to the widest possible horizons afforded by the time-charts of modern science and by our growing appreciation of the vast reaches and complexity of the homeliest acts. Nothing human is foreign to it.   No depths of misfortune or guilt elude it, and no wisdom or beauty is alien to it.

This new orthodoxy, experimental, reasonable, generous, and dauntless, furnishes hope for better understanding between different forms of faith.   It certainly cannot be content with mere tolerance of diverse systems.   Every serious form of religion is worthy of more than tolerance.   When its historical and cultural setting is properly appraised, each *cultus* gains a meaning which admits it to the great family of religions in its proper time and place. Existing faiths do not all belong to the present date on the calendar. Some are survivals. Others are beginnings. All have some appeal within their milieu. The social order is stratified with formations from different periods of time analogous to the various geological formations of the earth's surface. But increasing popular education, travel, and communication are creating a society of enlightened people over the world, eager for a form of religion in keeping with their enlightenment. The foreign students in any great university furnish an impressive illustration of this new cosmopolitan society.

The view which this book aims to express has practical bearing also upon the question of union among religious people. The Roman Catholic church is an illustration of the futility of attempting to comprehend all Christians under a rigid ecclesiasticism. Protestantism has repeatedly proved the impossibility of formulating a creed which can unify its sects. There remains the opportunity of undertaking to draw together at least the peoples of Western culture in a religious movement which is not primarily a creed or a priestly order but a method by which religious views of life and conduct may be freely fashioned and refashioned in keeping with new experience and enlarging faith.

The use of this method brings religion out of its muscle-bound rigidity into the freedom of vital growth and useful adaptation. If it thereby surrenders claims to absoluteness and finality, it yet gains concreteness and working power. This is what science has achieved for itself by its experimental, tentative use of hypotheses rather than by the assertion of fixed entities and eternal laws. The old demand for final definitions and iron categories has been given up in the domain of art much to its enrichment and serviceability. Carl Sandburg expressed this tendency in the realm of poetry by venturing to formulate thirty-eight definitions of poetry which were published in the *Atlantic Monthly*. Something like this loosening up of mind is needed with reference to the conception of religion. The following paragraphs illustrate the application of this principle to religion.

Of course there is no one definition of poetry. Nor is there any one statement of the nature of religion. The subject is so many sided that it will not be contained in any set formula, however carefully considered. It is like life itself—rich, iridescent, flowing, full of "depths, crypts, cross-lights, and moon-wisps." Let me then construct a few definitions of religion which had better be used as suggestions for making up other definitions endlessly, rather than as propositions to be committed to memory and adopted once for all.

Religion is living the best kind of life one can conceive with enthusiasm and trust.

Religion is the turning of the soul to God.

Religion is loving one's neighbor as one's self.

Religion is taking the world as a fairy land of beauty and love within sight of garbage dumps and fist fights.

Religion is the endeavor to move mountains with a wish of the heart or the whispering wings of hope.

Religion is a battle between a sword and a cross.

Religion is a quest for life in an abyss of death.

Religion is life among angels and demons with wireless signals of distress and comfort.

Religion is the loss of everything but courage.

Religion is a song and a prayer on a corner where street-car lines intersect and the cries of the news-boys mingle with the roar of the elevated.

Religion is marching with red banners and the blare of trumpets through muddy streets.

Religion is faith in a dead man nailed to a tree.

Religion is feasting on the dead man's flesh and drinking his blood.

Religion is claiming forgiveness beyond the stars for murder done here on the earth.

Religion is sitting together under a wind-blown roof and listening to the crooning hymns and the begging prayers of wistful souls.

Religion is living in imagination with a lot of Jews and with one Jew in particular.

Religion is a breath of daring silence in the din of angry clatter and profanity.

Religion is composure of soul when the ocean liner sinks.

Religion is the mirth of kindred spirits round a glowing fire with the shadows playing over a vacant chair.

Religion is dumb wonder under the starry sky and over the cradle of a babe.

Religion is the rapture of a timid heart in the light of the sun, or in the fragrance of a flower.

Religion is a corporation not for profit, producing wealth and offering it to paupers on condition of a bath.

Religion is a reform movement struggling against many obstacles a great number of which are imaginary.

Religion is a grand opera company singing the "Hallelujah Chorus."

Religion is the longing of a mother for a lost son when that longing turns into affection for other sons who have lost their mothers.

Religion is the soft warmth of a bird's wing and the cool shade of a tree.

Religion is an outlook from a mountain top with clouds floating below, making little gray patches on the widespreading plain in the distance.

Religion is the bond between the spring sowing and the autumn harvest.

Religion is the fiery furnace from which comes forth under the eye of grimy, perspiring men molten iron to be fashioned into steel beams and girders.

Religion is a view of a sleeping city at midnight when the moon is full.

Religion is a journey from Chicago's west side to

the lake front, or from New York's east side to
Broadway and back again, without loss of memory.

Religion is joy in the odor of ether in a hospital,
or of new-mown hay in harvest.

Religion is an adventure in the interior of China
or Tibet without guns or body-guards in search of
no plunder or concessions.

Religion is the bleaching of black souls white on
the shores of reflection and new deeds.

Religion is the preservation of childhood tender-
ness and trust with the experience and sorrow of
old age.

Religion is the bond of love encircling the earth
and binding the world to the heart of God.

People are frequently confused between
belief in God and theories about God.
There is no statement or formulation of his
nature which can satisfy all demands of the
intellect and the heart. A wealth of interests appear in the conceptions of God in the
most devout literature. In the Bible itself
there is no single, logical definition. God is
love. God is light. God is spirit. If such
assertions are taken freely, with the rich suggestions which they imply, then they are
useful and persuasive. But when they are
made the basis of hard and fast dogmas

they defeat the very ends of religion and lead to atheism and doubt as often as to faith and assurance. The main question about God for religion as an active, buoyant, outreaching participation in life is: Do you believe in God? Meaning: Do you trust life? Do you think there are some things better than others? Is it worth while to work for ideal causes, to sacrifice something of your comfort and peace of mind, to count yourself a co-worker with God? When you ask what kind of being God is, where he is, how old he is, how powerful he is, whether he created the world, whether he has made man immortal, whether he will punish the wicked in a fiery hell, while the righteous lie in celestial hammocks under shady fruit trees by cool streams, then you are asking questions which may call for speculative answers, but which may not have immediate practical religious value. It is not essential to a successful religion to have a consistent or even an intellectually satisfactory doctrine of God, as the history of religion shows.

But it is essential to believe in God in some sense, and to take definite attitudes on behalf of his government of the world. You may accept my faith in God without accepting my conception of his nature or of his relation to the world. I do not say that the faith can be the same in every respect where the doctrines differ, but I believe it can be for practical purposes.

The author would like to remind the reader that this book is the outgrowth not only of academic studies in the field of religion but also of many years of experience in the pastorate of a church. In the latter relation at least, the ideas here presented have been tested out in a very practical way. One evidence of the hearty response with which they have met is the fact that the church heartily indorsed and authorized the publication of the book. Since its first publication there have been increasing evidences that many thoughtful people find in some such statement satisfying answers to vital questions about religion.

E. S. A.

January 1, 1925

CONTENTS

CHAPTER   PAGE

I. THE NEW ORTHODOXY: ITS ATTITUDES   I

II. THE NEW ORTHODOXY: ITS DRAMATIS
       PERSONAE   29

III. THE NEW ORTHODOXY: ITS GROWING
       BIBLE   54

IV. THE NEW ORTHODOXY: ITS CHANGING
       GOAL   83

V. THE NEW ORTHODOXY: ITS NEW DRAMA   107

CHAPTER I

THE NEW ORTHODOXY: ITS ATTITUDES

Thoughtful people are aware that the opening decades of this twentieth century have already defined one of the most important epochs in history. The century was ushered in with a consciousness of progress and of new developments such as no other century has known. Everywhere were recounted the inventions, the discoveries, the revolutionary achievements in democaacy, in education, in the arts, in industry, and in religion. What was then clear to a few is now becoming familiar to the vast multitudes of laborers and peasants in every land. Social revolutions have written in blood and tears the end of the old and the beginning of the new. Industrial and political forces have wrought spectacular transformations in all human affairs. Airplanes, wireless messages, and

X-rays are no more wonderful or significant than rising democracy in China or the swelling tide of knowledge and power among the hitherto subject masses of all civilized countries. An abyss of measureless dimensions stretches between the old and the new epochs of man's life. It is not so much a distance of time as of interests and ideals. Looking back from the present across a score of years, how remote and diminished the old order seems! The majesty of its empires and the glitter of its royal courts drop into the same overwhelming gulf which has entombed giants and fairies and armored knights. Their authority has disappeared. Nothing of that vanished world commands the allegiance of men simply because it was part of that age. Only those things can be perpetuated which are renewed in the living experience of succeeding days. If it was once sufficient that spiritual values be proclaimed by prophets and priests, it has now become necessary that they shall be proved anew by each generation for itself.

For this new time, already begun for those who are truly at home in the twentieth century of the spiritual calendar of mankind, how shall the picture of man's life and destiny be drawn? They have thrown off the rule of superstition and the authority of kings and priests. They do not believe in miracles. Their world is not divided by the clouds into human and divine, nor by forms of dress or types of architecture into sacred and secular. Nor are they content with mere denial. Iconoclasm is not the mark of really modern men. They seek to build, to construct, to create. In place of dungeons of fear, irrational creeds, and magical rituals they are not content to leave only barrenness and doubt. New hopes, better doctrines, and more satisfying symbols are springing up out of the idealism and faith of the emancipated mind and heart. As in the sixteenth century the small earth-centered universe gave way to a cosmos of stellar spaces of incalculable magnitude, and as the little six thousand years of mundane existence

expanded into the hundreds of thousands
of years for the setting of the human
drama, so the simple picture of Bunyan's
Pilgrim's Progress has dissolved into the
gigantic struggle of hundreds of millions
of men over the whole earth to realize an
actual and visible society of righteousness,
justice, and love. The cravings of the
souls of men are no longer to be satisfied
with the dream of individual salvation after
this life in a walled town with jeweled gates
and flashing pavements, outside of which
in unending night and pain the infinitely
greater number of their fellow-men forever
wander, tortured and damned.

What religious conceptions are adequate
to the dawning day of our larger mental
and moral life ? Dare we hope that these
shall be found in the revival of some mys-
terious cult of the prescientific childhood of
the race—in theosophy or some oriental
mystery-religion ? Is it imaginable that
we are to be content with some pretentious
propaganda of healing which begins by
renouncing the very foundations of science

and the common-sense reality of practical experience? The refusal of minds of first rank to accept these religions cannot be offset by any number of devotees gathered from those who are not aware of the progress which has been made in the physical and social sciences. These movements do undoubtedly answer certain real needs of human nature and are obviously conducted by shrewd administrators and propagandists, but to suppose that they represent an adequate provision for the many-sided and profound claims of the human spirit is an illusion which time will expose.

There is more reasonable hope that the great historic development of religion represented by Christianity is destined to come to a new birth of power. This cannot be expected to occur, however, through a mere emotional revival of its traditional forms and doctrines. These have outlived the order of society in which they appeared and are already transcended by the leaders of religious thought still working within their domains. Such mighty social structures do not pass away at a stroke. It required centuries to build them, and they linger on in the world just as monarchies persist long after democracy has become the accepted political ideal of the world. Christianity has lived through three marked stages and, it is believed by many, is now entering upon a fourth. The first was its earliest form, in which it was a tremendously vital impulse to a higher, freer moral life among informal intimate groups, having their common bond in allegiance to the personality and inspiring message of Jesus of Nazareth. That period is directly reflected in our New Testament. Upon its pages are the fresh imprints of the vibrant, pulsing spirit of the Master. But there is little organization. It has been impossible for the most searching scholarship to find there a model for the conduct of the modern church. No fixed ritual is established. No clear and uniform body of doctrine is presented. No provision can be traced there for economic justice and social righteousness as needed by the twentieth century. But the moral aspiration and insight are there. The clear, commanding spiritual vision of Jesus shines through it as the rays of the rising sun illumine and warm the world. That record will therefore remain a source of inspiration to the end of time.

The second stage of Christianity was that known as Catholicism. It developed by the gradual extension of the faith to great numbers of communities throughout the Roman Empire and among barbarian tribes. Contact with Greek philosophy was also a great factor in formulating the conceptions of the early church. When Christianity permeated the empire it was inevitable that it should be affected by the Latin genius for organization and by the Greek power of reflective thought. The ecclesiastical institution known to us as the Roman Catholic church may truly be regarded as deriving its impetus from the gospels, its form from the Roman Empire, and its formulations of doctrine from Greek philosophy. The official authority which characterizes it is inevitably of the quality of the system on which it was patterned. This type of Christianity was arrested in its progress by the Protestant Reformation of the sixteenth century. Its fate is sealed with the death knell of monarchy and bureaucracy in all social relations—in the family, in education, and in industry. It has produced many beautiful souls. It has adorned our human world with marvelous cathedrals and pageants. It has lifted the imagination of millions from sordid and transient things to pure and lofty visions of faith. But it is not the form of religion for the modern man.

What then of Protestantism? It has now had four centuries of history. The celebration of the four hundredth anniversary of Luther's break with the Catholic church has been widely observed. He introduced great reforms which continue to exert a powerful influence. He gave the Bible to the people and made Christianity the religion of a book as it had never been before. He struck at the sharp separation of the sacred and the secular by opposing the celibacy of the clergy, by recognizing the state as an agency of God, and by dignifying common labor as having religious value. But the movement which he inaugurated became dogmatic and fixed and has not fulfilled his hopes. In Calvinism the doctrinal interest predominated and gave rise to creeds and confessions of faith which stand in the background of most of the evangelical churches today. Puritanism became austere and antagonistic to many natural and vital interests. It developed strength of conscience and determination of will, but lost breadth and the social graces and appreciation of the fine arts. Under all its differences Protestantism retained certain elements of Catholicism. It distrusted human nature; it emphasized the sacraments as essential means of grace; it clung to external authority, to the doctrines of the supernatural, and to a miraculous conversion of the natural human being in order to make him truly religious.

It is not impossible that future historians will regard Protestantism as coming to its close with the end of the nineteenth century as a vital, ascending type of religion. In that century several of the most characteristic principles of Protestantism were undermined by a larger knowledge of history and science. Protestantism was individualistic; the new order is social. It assumed the infallibility of the Bible, and that is no longer tenable. It exalted authority, and now there is no legitimate authority except that of experience. It denied that man is naturally religious, while it is commonly accepted today that man is incurably religious. We may well believe therefore that Christianity is entering upon a fourth great epoch, which has already been called by various names. It is referred to as the religion of the spirit, as social Christianity, and as the religion of democracy.

There is real need at the present time for statements of this latest form of Christianity created by the profound influences

working through many agencies toward a
richer life for all classes of men. What is
this religion of the twentieth century?
How shall we set forth the religious life as
it appears in the light of the discoveries of
the historians of religion, biblical students,
natural scientists, and social psychologists?
Let us think of ourselves as perfectly free
souls, unawed by any authority over us or
by any superstition within us, yet reverent
toward the things which experience has
taught us and eagerly in quest of clearer
perceptions of the ideal possibilities of life.
How does the religious life appear? How
shall we understand its attitudes, its dramatis personae, its growing Bible, its
changing goal, and its new drama of the
spiritual life? Some persons have difficulty in thinking of the Christian life in
this way, but no apologies are necessary for
identifying it with the religious life at its
best. Indeed, the Christian life may be
regarded as just life itself at its best. It is
not in exclusive opposition to plain goodness or to life as symbolized by Plato, or

Buddha, or Confucius. In our culture the highest religion is Christianity. It stands for the best in our civilization. Nothing is too good to be called Christian, and it is difficult to conceive of any good thing appearing in our experience which is fundamentally alien to the Christian way of life.

The attitudes treated here are those toward life as it unfolds naturally in simple human relations, those involved in our social complexes, and those which relate to our efforts to contribute to the fulness and beauty of the life of the world. These may be called the attitudes of reverence, of love, and of faith. These seem to be demanded by life as we experience it in the light of science and of the most ideal attainments. And these qualities are illustrated in the life of Jesus. The Christianity of our time begins with its own direct sense of values, finds them in life as it is, and estimates them on their own merit. When it discovers that Jesus viewed the world in the same way, it sees in him a companionable spirit and a helper in the task of noble living.

First, then, reverence for life. We have come to have profound respect for the laws of nature, for the way she works, and for the possibility of co-operating with her. It is the scientific habit of mind to sit down quietly and observe the facts, to view patiently the processes in the growth of plants and animals and in the development of society in order to understand them and control them. Nothing is allowed to come between the scientist and the facts. Jesus took the same unprejudiced, impartial attitude when he said to his disciples, "Ye shall know the truth and the truth shall make you free." The order and connection of things in the inner life were to him no less real than the relations which exist in the outer world. "Do men gather grapes of thorns or figs of thistles? A good tree cannot bring forth evil fruit, neither can a corrupt tree bring forth good fruit." It was this appeal to life itself which enabled the people to understand him so readily and to appreciate the moral lessons which he drew from their common occupations and daily experiences. He did not shrink from life. He came eating and drinking and entered into the natural and simple interests of his townsmen and friends. His moral precepts were largely direct observations of what he saw going on about him. "Judge not that ye be not judged, for with what judgment ye judge, ye shall be judged, and with what measure ye mete, it shall be measured to you again." In those words he was simply telling what he had observed and what any of us may observe every day. It was the same when he said, "Ask and it shall be given you; seek and ye shall find; knock and it shall be opened unto you." He probably had in mind some undaunted souls who persistently kept after worthy objects and finally obtained them against heavy odds. Jesus appears very near to us because he is so real and straightforward in his estimates. He has precisely the attitude of a modern man who looks over the pictures of life in the newspapers or at the movies and recognizes the folly of the fool and the wisdom of the wise. Generosity begets generosity, hardness invites hardness. They that take the sword shall perish by the sword.

He may be said to have confidence in his teaching just because so little of it is his own in any exclusive sense. The message which he gives is in no sense private. It is the declaration of things which are right at hand but which are overlooked and neglected. In this sense there is a certain identity between the teaching of Jesus and what is called paganism. The authority for what he teaches is found in the nature of the experience itself and may be verified by anyone. Even paganism in the sense of the joy of life, the delight in friendship and in nature and in humor and in the free play of the imagination, is not wanting. The great parables—the Prodigal Son, the Good Samaritan, the Wise and Foolish Virgins, the Sower and the Husbandman—are straight out of life and have traveled around the world for two thousand years

as true counterparts of actual conditions
in the lives of the people.   It did not re-
quire a special revelation to make them
true.   They would have been just as true
from any other lips.   Because he saw
people as they are, with their ideals as well
as their sins, and pictured them to themselves with such fidelity, he has won their
hearts and inspired their wills.

Religion is for him the maintenance of
this attitude of respect for life.   The divine
order is not different in principle from that
which we constantly observe.   God is like
a good shepherd seeking his lost sheep.   He
is like the father receiving back his prodigal
son.   The analogies of seedtime and harvest hold in the moral realm.   Whoever,
then, in our day has this reverence for life,
respects its simple principles of industry, of
generosity, of persistence, and of fidelity,
possesses in this respect the Christian attitude and is to that extent and by that very
fact a Christian.   The modern man gains
a new attachment for Jesus in this discovery, for there is here no longer the sense

of something artificial and arbitrary, but a common human response to the great spectacle of the world. In all that wonderful panorama some things appear better than others. The differences are as clear to the plain man as to the prophet when once they are pointed out. It is the function of the prophet to call attention to them, and it is the measure of his greatness that he is able to do so in such vivid pictures that men remember and have their wills stirred to act accordingly.

The great moral distinctions between good and bad, right and wrong, have arisen out of the long and tortuous experience of the race. Like language and art they have been fashioned first in the give and take of use and wont. Later they have been formulated and codified by prophets and social leaders. The conviction which a moral leader awakens is not due to what he brings with him so much as to the disclosures he makes concerning the habits which men already employ. He deals in typical cases: "A certain man had two

sons"; or "There was a certain rich man
which had a steward"; or "What man of
you having an hundred sheep, if he lose one
. . . ." In the time and country of Jesus
every man worth taking into account had
at least two sons, every rich man naturally
had a steward, and every farmer of any
significance had at least a hundred sheep.
The stories therefore had point and could
be verified with little difficulty. They de-
rived their significance not from the man
who told them but from life itself. His
glory was in his clear and illuminating insight which became so revealing and so
convincing the moment men compared
what he said with what they saw all about
them. He is vital for us now because he
lodged the authority of his word in what he
saw, in what all experienced, and in the distinctions which had been made before him
but which needed reinforcement through
such an energizing and convincing soul as
his. He accepted the Ten Commandments, but he knew they were not all of
equal importance and he did not hesitate

even in the presence of the formal teachers
of the Law to assert which was the greatest
and to put another beside it as of equal
value. The attitude of Christ toward life
was then one of reverence for its moral
distinctions and its ethical values. We
share that attitude with him. We also
look to life for its meaning and for direction, and because we agree in this reverence
for life we are to this extent Christian.

The second conspicuous attitude of the
Christian life which I mention is love, especially love of our fellow-men. We are having a great awakening in recent years with
reference to social justice. This is the
phrase which we have adopted to express
the development in institutions, and par-
ticularly in the state, of the attitude of consideration of our fellow-men. There never
was such care of children or so much insur-
ance of different kinds for all classes. The
ingenuity and skill of modern science has
been drafted into the service of health
and longevity. The energies of educators,
statesmen, and artists have been enlisted

in the quest for the efficiency and happiness of the common people. A new determination has grown into religious fervor to safeguard and enrich human life everywhere. A corresponding conscience has appeared concerning the evils which afflict the race— poverty, disease, ignorance, prostitution, intemperance, and war. Never has there been such effective opposition to war. Its waste and suffering, its profound and tragic destructiveness, never have been so little relieved by illusions of romance or aggrandizement. The motives which once sustained it are losing their appeal. A constructive, universal humanitarianism is emerging. Men do not wait to find that love of their fellows is a supreme ideal of Christianity before they follow it. The impressive fact is that they believe themselves to have found a principle which rests directly upon experience, one which carries its own justification in itself. And they are right. But it is identical with the feeling which Jesus had for his fellows just the same.

The business man adopts better methods for the protection of his employees. He may have mixed motives about it, but one very real factor is his sense of friendliness for those who work with him and who are therefore neighbors to him. At least one of the discoveries made by agencies for the promotion of the welfare of employees is the genuine human interest taken by the employers when they understand the facts. Their attention has too often been centered upon other things in the conduct of business, but when they come into closer human relations with the men they are more and more ready to improve working conditions. Neighborliness is in reality dependent upon something more than physical proximity, as we who dwell in city apartments well understand. It is more than a formal connection with the machinery and the pay-roll of a firm. It is a question of fellow-feeling, of sympathetic imagination. It is a sense of having our interests intimately bound up together. It is a realization of comradeship in a common

cause.   Neighbors are not really neighbors
until their children play and quarrel together, or until they confer about paving
the alley, or until they are visited by common bereavement, or their sons go to war.
When these things happen, then love arises
between them; that is, good feeling, kindliness, mutual concern, spring up naturally
and of course.   The great improvements
in social adjustments are now being
brought about by using this simple fact.
In order to preserve our cities from im-
pending isolation of individuals in a great
maze of inhuman solid pavements and
brick walls, we have created parks and
playgrounds where the natural impulses to
play and to social contact may find satisfaction.

Nothing has helped more to create the
religious virtue of love to our fellow-men
in the cities than these places of association.   Formerly we left the development
of this Christian quality too much to the
saloon and the public dance hall!   It is one
of the most significant forward steps in our

society that we have begun to find out how to create the normal and natural conditions out of which the highest moral qualities can most successfully be produced. We have always believed, theoretically at least, that men should love each other, and we knew that under certain conditions they always did love each other, but we have only recently put these two things together and begun to create vast plans for the conditions under which a wider and firmer affection may spontaneously develop. Settlement workers, friendly visitors for the united charities, comrades in barracks and in the trenches, as well as classmates in college and members of the family, have found that the old injunction to love your neighbor means, when translated into experience, to live together, to share hardship and pleasure, storms and sunshine, tears and laughter, poverty and prosperity. It has been said that all face-to-face groups are naturally Christian. This conviction impels us to the conclusion, therefore, that what is needed is to bring the world face to face, and that is being accomplished in our time in unexpected ways. Travel and communication and the movies and other devices enable even the plainest citizen to enter into intimate understanding with classes and conditions which have hitherto been inaccessible to him. It is because this attitude of love which is central in the Christian conception is spontaneous and inevitable in life itself that it is not to be regarded as a fantastic dream that the world may continue increasingly to find itself and to call itself Christian.

The third attitude of the religious life is faith. Faith is that quality by which pioneers like Abraham and the Klondike adventurers go forth into new countries. It was the attitude of Columbus. It is the forward-striving, hopeful, expectant quality. To have faith means to be willing to take some risk for a cause. It is of the essence of business enterprise and of the creative spirit in science and in art. Religious faith means to have that feeling about life as a whole. No one is able to prove conclusively that human progress will continue, but no man can get the most out of life who refuses to believe in progress and in the possibility of improving the world.   In spite of all the lions in the way we must go on.   In spite of human frailties and weaknesses, in spite of follies and irrationalities, in spite of selfishness and greed, in spite of false ideals and paralyzing indifference, we must go on with our task whether it is our business, our science, our politics, or our religion.   They are all of a piece in this respect.   Everywhere we work against difficulties and in the face of discouragements which would be heartbreaking if we thought only of them.   But everywhere we keep hoping and fighting and believing that improvement is to be made.   When we give up that faith, we are done with life, or at least with that particular part of it concerning which we have lost faith.

This, too, is a natural attitude which has come to have a new appraisement.   The cults of cheerfulness which have sprung up on every hand witness to the response which this quality gains wherever it appears. That is one great factor in the irresistible charm of youth. In its normal state it is buoyant, believing, and undaunted. Here again it has been discovered that this spiritual quality of life has relation to practical and to physical conditions. As between a healthy man and an invalid, the healthy man will usually have the most faith and courage for the future. Therefore every means of banishing disease from the world may be regarded as a means of increasing our faith. Poverty and ignorance also depress and tend to break the spirit and contract the soul. Remunerative occupation and better education of the mind therefore become factors in the spiritual life.

But it is also true that faith is contagious. You must know that from the way in which salesmen and promoters communicate to you their enthusiasm for their goods and stocks. It is true, too, with reference to the ideal things of religion. It

is heartening to meet great souls like Jesus and Paul and Luther and Bishop Brooks, who are resilient and full of faith in the progress of the kingdom of love in the world. They look over the long distances which the race has traveled and are able to see savagery pass away and barbarism disappear, the old nomadic life of Israel give place to the kingdom, the old superstitions of magic and sorcery vanish before increasing intelligence, old cruelty surrender to kindliness, and the littleness of broken and scattered societies grow into the beauty and power of ordered states and empires. The Christian attitude of faith is that the world has immense possibilities and that these may be realized through the industry, intelligence, and good-will of men working in harmony with the highest knowledge and deepest convictions they possess.

These, then, are the attitudes of the religious life. Reverence for life and for the moral distinctions which commend themselves to the experience of the race; love for our fellow-men as the natural attitude of good-will and comradeship which arises wherever men really know and understand each other; and the forward-moving action of life in the quest for better things than have yet been achieved—these are the attitudes of the Christian life, and they are the attitudes of life itself at its best.   Is it too much to hope that one day this identity will be fully realized and that then it will be seen that wherever reverence and love and faith abound there also the Christian life has come to its own?   It is in this spirit that men are gaining a new appreciation of religion and a new and truer vision of Jesus Christ.   Instead of being dwarfed by the world's realization that his religion is the religion of life at its best, that discovery exalts him into a more intimate and persuasive leadership which invites new enthusiasm and devotion.

CHAPTER II

THE NEW ORTHODOXY: ITS DRAMATIS PERSONAE

Religion as we know it in our society is concerned with persons. This is a distinguishing feature. In the earlier stages of man's groping life he attached more importance to what are for us mere animals and material objects than he did to human beings. His ceremonials centered in the things around him. Often it was his food. At times it was a mountain or a stream. His deities were rice or maize, sheep or kangaroos, or any other objects acutely connected with his wants and his satisfactions. For long ages he cherished such things more than he did his own human kind. It is still true in some countries that animals are treated with more consideration than men and especially than women. Sometimes our western civilization is accused of valuing its machines higher than the lives of the men who run them. But in spite of all exceptions and of all failures to live up to it, the motto everywhere displayed is "safety first" for human beings. We are rapidly making this devotion to human welfare religious. It is only recently that negro slavery was abolished, and now agitation grows against the slavery of women, wage-slavery, and all forms of the subordination of men, women, or children to unjust or merely impersonal interests. Not only must they be freed from various kinds of bondage, but movements are under way to give them the resources of a larger human existence by means of education, better economic conditions, and larger opportunities for recreation, social contact, and genuine freedom.

The conservation of the race has come to be recognized as more important than the conservation of timber and minerals. This is no longer merely a sentiment, but it is embodied in laws and institutions. Not only do men exist for the state, but the state exists for men. At last man's understand-

ing of himself has become clear enough for
him to see that his highest duty is toward
his own kind, and that unless the life of
man himself is becoming larger and finer
nothing else can yield enduring satisfaction.   This is the meaning of the wars for
freedom and for conscience.   The heroes of
liberty and democracy have thought of
nothing as comparable in importance with
the nurture and enrichment of the spirit of
man.

This love of man toward man is cherished for no other reason than that it seems
the only natural and human attitude.   It
yields its own rewards.   As a father scorns
the thought that his love for his son needs
any command to stimulate it or any hope
of reward to keep it alive, so thousands who
have caught the social vision of our time
labor for better laws, better schools, better
recreations without waiting for a text of
Scripture to tell them that this is their duty
and without expecting any other compen-
sation than just that of seeing these results
accomplished.   Gradually it is becoming

apparent that this was precisely the attitude which dominated the mind and will of
Jesus.   Therefore leaders of social, humani-
tarian reforms find themselves in full accord with his spirit and ideals.   They have
come to have the same interest in building
a society that shall minister to the deepest
human wants.   Often they have found this
ideal by direct dealings with human needs,
much as he himself found it.   Therefore
a new sense of comradeship is springing up
between them and him, for they are fellow-
workers in the same great cause.   It is not
necessary to decide whether Jesus was the
first to have this attitude.   Nor is it vital
to know just how far he is responsible for
this feeling wherever it appears at the
present time.   We have come to know it
as the Christian view of life, and we think
of it as Christlike no matter in whom it is
manifest.   The religious life therefore in-
volves one's own personality, the personality of others, and of God.   These are the
dramatis personae.   In a history of religion it would be necessary to take account

of angels and demons, demigods and in-
numerable tribal deities. Here it is sufficient to interpret the self and other souls,
including Jesus Christ, the church, and
God. These are as intimately related to
one another as the members of a family.
Each must be seen in relation to the rest.
No one of them liveth unto himself.

Self is the word now more commonly
used than soul or spirit. It is the mind as
it knows itself. When one says "I" or
"me" or refers to himself by name, he des-
ignates the self. The description of one's
own personality is peculiarly difficult, but
the sense of it is most intimate and vital.
The psychologists have made great efforts
to make it clear, but with all their training
and practice they have not satisfied themselves. Professor James made a notable
contribution to the description and understanding of the self, and all writers upon the
subject go back to him for help. He cites
the case of Peter and Paul, who talk over
the events of the day just before they fall
asleep. Each understands the other and

each enters into the other's moods. They keep their own selves distinct, however. No confusion occurs between them when they wake in the morning. Each takes up his own train of ideas and connects with the events of the previous day without uncertainty as to whether he is recalling his own or the other's feelings. The basis of this recognition of his own state and of himself is in each case just the peculiar "warmth and intimacy" which one feels for some ideas or actions and not for others. Out of the stream of the conversation of the night before some attitudes and emotions are recalled which are welcomed at once as belonging to one's own inner world. In contrast to them the attitudes and emotions of the other person are more remote, colder, and carry no sense of possession.

The self is the being any man experiences himself to be. He is known to himself immediately in the sense of being at home with his thoughts and feelings. His own moods and memories are more familiar,

more urgent and alive. The self may un-
dergo sudden and extreme changes and yet
retain the feeling of being the same person.
The changes are just as real as the same-
ness. We are actually different from mood
to mood. It is astonishing how profoundly
the sense of ourselves may be affected by a
cup of coffee, a breath of fresh air suddenly
let into a stuffy room, a refreshing night's
sleep, success at a favorite game.

When I fall in with a stranger in a rail-
way coach, it is this actual self which is dis-
closed to him. He begins by remarking
that the weather is unusual for the time of
year. I give him a courteous but general
reply. He then refers to the football score
of the previous day, and I am all anima-
tion, volunteering remarks about a certain
team whose players I know and whose
records are forthwith reviewed. Later the
evening paper is thrust before us by the
newsboy, and the headlines are appeals
met by varying degrees of zest and attention. If we journey far and become com-
municative, we thus become aware of the

nature of the self possessed by each one.
His self is that of a traveling salesman dealing in rubber. He is well developed with
reference to automobile tires, rubber boots,
water hose, their uses, prices, and possible
substitutes. Socialism is his political
creed. His heart is wrapped up in a ten-
year-old daughter whose studies and play
and pets have forced him to attend to a
new world of things essential to the life of a
little girl. The conversation reveals by
many allusions and exclamations, stories
and passing references, the outline of his
inner world. I remark afterward that I
became acquainted with Mr. Smith during
that journey. It is literally true. His
personality stood forth in his very vocabulary and gestures. At some questions of
mine he would return quick answers with
eagerness, while to others he would merely
say indifferently that he did not know.
Occasionally, as when he mentioned his
little girl, one could observe an almost
tragic tension, as if his very heart rose and
beat in his words with anxiety and tense

affection. He followed none of my hints
about Schopenhauer or chess or South
America, knew nothing of Bret Harte, and
cared nothing for Airedale dogs. It was
not difficult to see that his self was highly
developed on the side of business and dis-
closed depths of fatherly pride in his
daughter, but was quite lacking in appreciation of poetry and conventional religion.

It is in some such way that the practical
person, whether he be scholar or man of
affairs, understands the self. He knows it
best of all in his own experience. He understands what it is to be perplexed and
depressed over his mistakes and misfor-
tunes, and also what it is to be elated over
success. If religion could talk to him in
terms of those experiences, he could understand it. It is this self which has to be
reckoned with first of all. Whether religion is vital depends on whether it is a
warm and powerful interest to this self
which is also concerned with business and
home and pleasure. The measure of a
man's interest in religion may be truly seen

in the time and thought he gives to it, in the response he makes to it in conversation, in the courage and patience with which he seeks to understand it in his reading and reflection.

Jesus realized that when men are most serious and honest with themselves they count their ideal moral interests of the greatest importance. When it comes to a test, all realize that "a man's life consisteth not in the abundance of the things which he possesseth." If it is a conflict between one's comfort and one's honor, the average man knows at once how to choose. Few men will betray their country for bribes. There is a recognized hierarchy of values which puts material goods on the lowest and spiritual things on the highest plane. When forced to choose, men do not fear those who can merely destroy the body, but fear rather those who strike at liberty and justice. There is consequently urgent meaning in the question, "What shall it profit a man if he shall gain the whole world and lose his own soul"—his larger and nobler self? Religion magnifies this better self for which men are willing to sacrifice everything else.

One of the characteristics of this self is that it has no independent being but is intimately and organically bound up with others. It is a common observation that a single child in a home is at a very real disadvantage as compared with one who has brothers and sisters. The conditions for growth of personality lie in the give and take of the interaction of many individuals. If a human infant could be kept alive and brought to years of maturity without contact with other human beings, it is difficult to imagine how pitiful and inhuman his state would be. He would be without language and would have few, if any, of the abilities which set man apart from the lower animals. A distinctively human self would be lacking in him. By the same principle the more vital relations a person has with the developed human world the larger self or personality he gains. Therefore other friendly persons are indispensable conditions of the religious life. They constitute the family group within which one is nourished, protected, and fashioned. In its early days the church was sometimes identical with a household. It is not an accident that the terms denoting the domestic life hold over into the larger body. The members of the church have the same intimate feeling for each other. They call themselves brothers and sisters. They exercise brotherly care and affection and discipline. Misunderstandings of the nature and function of the church would often be avoided if it were more commonly thought of in terms of this natural family relation. It would be seen to be less formal and more intimate, nearer and more pliable in its action upon its members. This encompassing body becomes a kind of corporate personality. One feels loyalty toward it and protects its good name. Through a sense of participation in its larger, more stable life the individual comes to consciousness of himself and of it. The church was in early Christian society, and in its

less formal types is today, more nearly
what the old clan group was to its members—an intimate association, sustaining
and controlling them without the narrow-
ness and antagonism of the circumscribed
clan. Every interest of the local church
tends to carry the intimacy and affection of
its inner life out to the larger invisible
church universal of which it feels itself a
part. In the literature of the early Christians that tendency was marked. The references to the grace of hospitality are fre-
quent. When they traveled into distant
cities they were often cared for in the
homes of their comrades in the faith to
whom they were otherwise entire strangers.

The church became to the apostle Paul
one organic body, mystical and spiritual,
yet real, within which the individual felt
himself upborne and nurtured. So vivid
was this wholeness and spiritual unity for
him that he thought of it as one being, a
person, the bride of Christ. For her devout sons the church is a great life running
through the centuries, constituted of all

those who have participated in her faith and work. In her are included all the noble company of the apostles, heroes, martyrs, and saints who have shared in her labors and hopes. They merge into her growing soul and form that vast communion in whose fellowship the Christian renews his sense of the reality of the Kingdom of Heaven.

Often, in the past, the church has seemed to stand in sharp contrast to other institutions. For many centuries Christianity awakened the scorn and then the fear and opposition of the older order. To the Christians the governments, the armies, the wealth, and most of the comforts of life appeared to belong, not to them, but to the world. Christianity became a thing apart and remains so in its inner feeling and attitude to this day among the vast majority of its followers. They do not yet really believe that it is possible for a man to be both a citizen of this world and a citizen of the heavenly kingdom without inconsistency and tragic conflict. In spite of her victory over the temporal powers, the Catholic church never came to the point where she could trust herself to live in the world. To this day she remains apart, celibate and otherworldly, mystical and ascetic, through the conviction that the life of the spirit is fundamentally incompatible with the natural order. All other Christian bodies have been deeply infected with that despair of this world. Therefore there yet remains over against the traditional Christian the traditional worldling. This worldling is one of the dramatis personae. He is a less lively figure in the imagination now than in the past, though he still gives color and contrast to the fading picture. He is gaily dressed. He employs the arts, is convivial and human. He was as repugnant to the puritan as to the old ascetic. In modern religion he isn't so bad. If he is merely a pleasure-seeker, without serious purpose, he falls under the judgment that he is useful neither to himself nor to society. His way of living carries its own condemnation, for it does not yield the solid satisfactions of larger participation in the affairs of the community.

We are finding out, however, new uses for leisure, for art, for play, and for wealth. Here we are in deeper accord with Jesus than with his mediaeval or puritanical followers. He moved in the midst of the stream of human life, amused and stirred as well as angered and amazed that men should be so blind and wasteful of their opportunities. The traditional contrast between the saints and the sinners, between the saved and the lost, does not hold in its familiar form. Those terms belonged to a static and fixed system in which it was thought one must be either all of one or all of the other. As a matter of fact, the Christian life is a growth, and those who participate in it are not altogether perfect, nor are those who do not profess it altogether bad. There is much that is bad in the best of us, and there is a great deal of good in the worst of us. Some people in the churches have tendencies which, if unchecked, would take them to the penitentiary, while some convicts in prisons would probably make good mayors of cities or good editors of newspapers. The prison walls are not coterminous with the bounds of sin and virtue, nor are the walls of the churches the sharp dividing line. Human life is mixed in all men. That which entitles one to be called a good man is not perfection but fairly reliable desires and habits for doing the right thing, and that which classifies one as bad is his perverse desires and habits, which tend to get him into trouble and to lead to defeat. In such a state society cannot be perfect either. Like the individuals in it, it is mixed, and may be considered good or bad in terms of its tendencies and its fruits.

Three of the most important of the dramatis personae remain for consideration. Usually they are referred to as the three persons of the Trinity, the meaning of which word has never been made clear. The doctrines of the Trinity have little significance in our time. They are not

demanded by our moral life and they are not
taught by the Scriptures. Therefore they
may be allowed to pass with the intellectual world to which they belonged. If it
were necessary to treat of Jesus in relation
to the Trinity the modern theologian
would have little to say except what concerns the history of that conception. For
himself it has little meaning. But of Jesus
there is much to say. The impression of
his life is so natural and convincing in the
New Testament that there is little force in
the contention that he never lived. Even
the stories relating to his birth and his
death are such as might easily have grown
up among his followers in that age without
any intention to deceive or misread the
facts. Those stories are the expression of
the boundless love and admiration of men
who believed him utterly divine. They are
the record of the wonder-love of the human
heart, which continues to make legend-
ary narratives about very human men.
It has happened to Abraham Lincoln,
who lived in the full light of a scien-

tific era and died little more than a half-
century ago. The figure of Jesus as a
moral teacher and as a courageous freeman
against the background of hard conven-
tion and narrow prejudice is becoming
more distinct and more moving. There is
no doubt that fine souls have been turned
from him by the artificial and preposterous
claims of many of his followers. But now
that it is possible to understand him more
directly and to assess his mind and message more adequately, he is gaining a new
hold upon the will and the affection of all
classes. If it were only the educated
classes who were discovering the power of
his personality, it would not be so significant, but there are signs that the masses of
men are coming to realize better how near
he is to them and how sincerely he speaks
to the heart of the common people. His
words remain unique and vital in religion
as those of Shakespeare do in literature
or of Plato in philosophy. He moves to
the heart of moral issues with the sure,
swift insight of clear thought and of pure

impulse. He speaks out of life and by constant reference to it almost like an empirical scientist of today. This fundamental note is so clear that it becomes a touchstone in connection with scholarly studies for deciding the genuineness of doubtful passages. Nor is it difficult to believe that this urgent religious enthusiasm for moral ideals will keep him supreme among the religious leaders through the ages. He will continue to be the living companion of those who come to know him, and the charm of his personality will continue to radiate itself through the world.

The Holy Spirit in the history of the church came into prominence after the death of Jesus. He was the Comforter who arose in the thought of the early disciples when they were bereft. He was an unseen presence felt whenever they came together and opened their hearts to one another. To him they attributed the words which they spoke in moments of peril before judges and accusers or at times of elation in the assembly of the church. It is not impossible to identify the experience out of which this personality arose. It is recognized in the sense of companionship we have felt in the uplifting moments of great gatherings or when moved by an overmastering impulse to utter the truth as we see it. Colonel Francis Younghusband, of the English expeditionary forces to Tibet, tells of his experience when wounded and ill in the hospital in Llhassa. He felt borne up by the physicians and the nurses and by the atmosphere of sympathy and comfort which they created around him. The spirit of this group of friends and helpers became to him the Holy Spirit. He said to a friend, "In those days the God who was most real to me was not God the Father; nor God the Son; but God the Holy Spirit."

This experience expresses the tendency of many discerning souls in their thought of God. He is no longer sought outside the world in unattainable distances of the unknown and unknowable. Nor is he

approached primarily through physical nature.   He is found in the associated life of
men, especially when that association is
aspiring and productive.   Men are at their
best when striving for fuller life, for more
adequate knowledge, and a larger measure
of justice.   God is love; the serving, suffering, healing love which binds men together
in nations and kindreds and leagues of
peace for the common good.   Every constructive, fruitful organization of people is
a means of understanding the divine.   It
is not an accident that we think of great
social entities as great personalities.   Our
college is our Virgin Mother, to whom we
address songs and sentiments of genuine
affection.   Our city has a personality,
photographed and visualized, whenever
her honor or her ambition is challenged.
Each state has an individuality and every
nation is personified through a definite face
and figure.   Is it not just as natural to
sum up the meaning of the whole of life in
the person and image of God ?   Seemingly
it is equally inevitable.   It appears to be

the most natural and the simplest way to represent to our minds and wills the moral values and the spiritual realities of life. Our own selves have grown up through interaction with other selves both sensible and ideal. In our private reflections we carry on conversations with people present to our imaginations who are none the less important and influential with us when they are not physically tangible and visible. God is the great Ideal Companion. To commune with him is to gain new appreciations of all that he signifies to us. He is then identified with Strength and Wisdom and Nobility. To be loyal to him is to strive to adhere to all that he means to us.

To develop the familiar image of a parent or friend or historical character to the point where it serves as the most vivid symbol of the divine is doubtless a common experience. "The light of the knowledge of the glory of God in the face of Jesus Christ" is the great reality to Christians. The warmth and comfort and contentment which Christianity affords may be found

largely in that fact. In him God comes
near and takes the form we can grasp and
utilize. In practical religious life men
easily feel themselves in the presence of
God when they recall his face. This is not
due so much to any theological conviction
about the doctrine of his divinity as it is
to long training and practice in associating
Christ with all that they feel and respect
as divine.

These persons of the religious drama
cannot be separated from each other.
They are bound up together in an intimacy
as vital as that which unites the members
of an organism. No one of them can
live without the others nor without the
whole. The self grows through interplay
with the selves around it. It could not
exist without them. Over and above the
particular persons constituting one's class
or country or world is the feeling of the
entity of the class or country or world
itself. Each class in a school possesses an
individuality to which the members manifest loyalty and reverence. That indi-

viduality has a certain objectivity and per-
manence above and beyond any particular
persons within it.   In a sense it transcends
them.   Yet that individuality obviously is
in and through them.   If this be the nature
of God as the Ideal Socius, then he too has
at least such reality and objectivity.   He
is the Soul of the world in which all other
selves live and move and have their being.

CHAPTER III

THE NEW ORTHODOXY: ITS GROWING BIBLE

One of the striking facts in the religious experience of the modern man is that while he seems to hold sacred things more lightly than did the passing generation, yet in reality he cherishes those to which he does cling with a more vital faith. He is discovering that religion does not need to be defended and protected in order to preserve it in the world. It has a surprising depth and persistence. The rationalistic mind of the eighteenth and nineteenth centuries, which still survives here and there in societies and individuals designating themselves as rationalists, assumed that religion could not survive criticism. They supposed that religion was so inextricably bound up with superstition and supernaturalism that when these were exposed and cast aside religion itself would perish.

This too has been the conviction of the extreme conservatives. They must believe the Bible "from cover to cover" or reject it all. If they should relax their adherence to miracle or prophecy they could not believe in the veracity of the teaching. There is thus a significant likeness between the extremes. They agree that one must accept all or nothing. No discrimination or qualification is approved. The Bible and the Christian religion are to be defended or rejected *in toto*.

The man of the modern mind, trained in history and in the social sciences, takes a different view. He does not indorse all that has been claimed for the Bible nor does he take it to be of equal worth in all its parts. Yet he finds in it messages of greatest value. Even contradictions, discrepancies, superstitions, and myths may be discovered without weakening the force of the moral ideals and precepts. Those things which are self-evidencing and verifiable in experience cannot be deprived of their validity because of accompanying errors or misconceptions. Religion is at last seen to be greater than the traditions which have grown up with it. It has deeper springs in human nature than have been suspected. Instead of being a delicate and tender growth it proves to be hardy and vigorous. Therefore it does not have to be sheltered and hidden against investigation and criticism. It cannot thrive at its best under patronizing influences nor at the hands of those who are unwilling to trust it to the free play of social forces. Certainly many men in our time have been surprised to realize how much more vital and satisfying their religious faith became the moment they began to view it with the same freedom and intelligence with which they regard art and politics. As with all other big human concerns, religion is at its best where it is close to life, unhindered by authority and open to reasonable, sympathetic criticism. Again and again in the history of Christianity its vital force has broken through old forms and doctrines and created new symbols and types of service. The dogma of biblical infallibility is one of the artificialities recently discarded, and the result has been the strengthening of religion.

One of the best correctives for mistaken and exaggerated views of any phase of religion is the study of its history. When the Bible is viewed from the beginning of the church through the changing centuries, many things concerning it are made plain. The word "Bible" gets a new meaning. It is no more a single book but a collection of books. The proper translation of the Greek from which the word "Bible" comes is "the books." That fact alone lessens the impression of singleness and unity which has prevailed. The Bible means a collection of writings, a little library of sixty-six books. These are all printed separately by the American Bible Society at one penny each, and it might be an aid to the right use of them if they were always sold separately rather than being bound together in flexible bindings so different from other books. It is even an occasion

of comment to be seen carrying a copy of
the Bible on the street, especially on any
other day than Sunday, because it is still
felt to be different from other books, and
those who carry it are looked upon as not
quite natural and human.

The fact that the Bible is not one but
many books is clear from the history of the
selection of the writings contained in it.
It is difficult for us to realize that the Bible
has not always meant just the words
brought together in our Oxford editions.
Few people stop to think that the early
church did not have any of the writings of
the New Testament until the latter part
of the first century, and then only in the
informal and uncompilated form of letters
and sayings circulated from hand to hand
and by word of mouth. Yet it is of profound importance to realize that the church
is older than its written documents and was
the cause of them. Naturally today the
book is regarded as the seed from which
churches spring, and the common impression easily arises that it was always so, but

originally the opposite was the case. The first disciples had, of course, only the Scriptures of the Old Testament, and these were in different versions, lacking uniformity as to the number and character of the constituent books. It was late in the fourth century before a list of the New Testament books appeared which is identical with our own. Before that time there was a very notable variation. The oldest parts of our New Testament are the letters of Paul. These began to be written about twenty years after the death of Jesus. They were not prepared for publication, much less as permanent documents. They were concerned with problems in local churches and with the conduct and spiritual needs of individuals, and were passed around among interested friends in much the same way as letters today from one on a journey.

Our New Testament contains twenty-seven books, but Justin Martyr in the middle of the second century mentions only thirteen or fourteen. Irenaeus, about

185 A.D., speaks of twenty-one. A list
from about 200 A.D., known as the Mura-
torian Canon, contains twenty-four, among
which are the Revelation of Peter and the
Wisdom of Solomon. The author of this
list frankly says that some would also include other books, and names the Shepherd
of Hermas, but he would not include them.
He accepts the Apocalypse of Peter as well
as the Revelation of John which we have.
But he does not have the Epistles of Peter,
nor the third letter of John, nor the Epistle
of James. Throughout this period and
until the time of the Reformation there was
never so much importance attached to the
inspiration and authority of these writings
as we are accustomed to ascribe to them.
When individual Christians sought counsel
and instruction they went to the church
itself, to the congregation of believers or
to the leaders, such as the presbyters or
bishops. Until the age of Luther the
church was the recognized source and
medium of authority. The group itself
settled its problems and furnished guid-

ance for its members. The congregations clearly held the writings of Scripture in high esteem, but they did not regard them as the sole nor the supreme means of ascertaining the truth. The spirit of the church itself was the real court of appeal. This conviction continued into Reformation times, and was only obscured by the reaction against abuses by the hierarchy of the Roman church. Martin Luther himself, with all his devotion to the Bible, did not receive all of the books as of equal value, but went so far as to reject the letter of James as "an epistle of straw" and the Revelation of John as of doubtful right to a place in the canon. He did not include the Revelation in his version of the Scriptures but printed it in an appendix with Hebrews, James, and Jude.

Apparently the event which fixed the Bible in the form in which we know it was the official publication of the King James translation, commonly known as the Authorized Version. It was the first authoritative translation of the whole

Bible into any modern vernacular language. It was made by the King's command. He was the head of the church in England, and it was appointed by him to be read in the churches. The reverence felt for the Bible was greatly augmented by this translation. It gained prestige and became of increasing interest to the people. It was, however, too expensive to be purchased generally, and the majority were too illiterate to read it. It remained, therefore, in the hands of the clergy to a large extent and was known chiefly to the public through being read in the services of the churches. By the natural tendency already fostered through the authority of the state and the church and by the importance attached to it by the preachers among the common people, the book came to be regarded with a feeling of awe and superstitious devotion. Perhaps it was the work of the British and other Bible societies which did most to make it accessible and at the same time to transform it into a kind of popular fetish. Before the organization of these societies the Bible was a luxury which few could afford. In the sixteenth century, the time of Shakespeare, the Bible was so rare as to be possessed only by the few, while for the use of those who could not buy it a copy was chained to a reading desk in the cathedrals where the people could have access to it and at the same time not be able to steal it.

The Bible Society changed all this by printing the book in vast editions. Gifts of charity were secured for its wider circulation. The response to the appeal of the society on behalf of the poor to whom it sought to distribute Bibles was greater than any appeals for those suffering from famine and pestilence. In the middle of the nineteenth century the society distributed half a million a year and increased its output until its presence in the households of the common people in civilized lands and in countries reached by missionaries has become one of the amazing phenomena of the age. The faith thus displayed in the power of the Bible without note or comment to transform the world is a striking illustration of the miraculous influence attributed to it. Along with the book went the belief in its complete inspiration and in its efficacy to convert the souls of its humblest readers. We should not marvel that it was regarded as a sacred object, whose presence brought safety to the home and the daily reading of which accumulated merit for the soul. It is hardly a mere coincidence that the period of its greatest circulation has been the time of the deepest and most widespread belief in its infallibility and uniqueness. Many people still believe that they can at any moment receive from it a divine message for any perplexity on the first page opened at random.

The fact that this extreme view of the supernatural and infallible character of the Bible is so recent and so much the belief of the less educated classes should prepare us to understand the modern view without confusion or distrust. The first step in the appreciation of what is meant by the growing Bible is to realize that the conception of it as a complete and final revelation is exceptional in the history of the church and is characteristic of a short period of time which is now passing away. The older and profounder belief that God has not left himself without witness among any people and that he has his living prophets in every age has found new expression through the most authentic spirits of our time. There is no need to deny to the first Christian century and the writings of the early disciples a certain uniqueness and compelling directness. They have the quality of the first fresh impulse and urgent moral appeal of the personal impress of Jesus and Paul and their immediate companions. What they said and wrote stands apart as the record of an epoch distinct from any before or after it. Nowhere is it duplicated, nor is it likely to be. On this account its canon of documents naturally becomes fairly well defined. They were the expression of a definite personal history and its influence upon certain characters and institutions of the time. As that age passed into history its outline took shape and remains clear among all the epochs of man's spiritual struggle. So well marked are its spirit and its word that it is possible to determine whether newly discovered writings really belong to it, and indeed whether specific lines and words traditionally embodied in the oldest extant manuscripts are genuine portions of the Christian message. There is some possibility that discoveries are yet to be made of letters or gospels purporting to belong to that message. If such should appear, their indicated date and authorship would not be so decisive in determining their genuineness as would their contents and their correspondence with that which is already known as authentic.

The problem of establishing the body of writings which belong to the church of the first century is not radically different from that of selecting the great literary products of any other well-defined period, such as the golden age of Greece or the Elizabethan

era of English history. The scholars in
these fields are conscious of a collection of
writings just as characteristic, just as organic, as the collection which we know as
the Bible. The latter is the product of the
religious life of the Hebrew people and its
full bloom in Christianity. Those records
and messages which constitute the Scriptures or writings of that stream of human
experience are said to be inspired, inspiration here being equivalent to distinctness
or separateness. But the fact is usually
overlooked that the selection of writings which are "inspired" was determined
finally long after the time of their appear-
ance. This has certainly been true of the
canon of Scripture. By the same principle
it might be appropriate to say that certain
books belong to the canon of Greek literature, namely, those which bear the impress
of the Greek genius as shown by their participation in a certain body of characteristic ideas and attitudes. These are the only
works which are truly inspired by that
genius. They are unique and inimitable.

That canon also is closed. It has been finished and sealed.

In similar manner one may regard the written records of any age. The Elizabethan era of English letters embraces a definite list of authors, the great names of which are Spenser, Shakespeare, and Bacon. The lesser lights are Ben Jonson, Marlowe, Beaumont, and Fletcher, with others like Lodge and Sidney and numerous anonymous authors making up the chorus and background. These all have a certain kinship in their problems and outlook and general philosophy of life. The same is true of the Victorian writers, Tennyson, Browning, Matthew Arnold, and their lesser kin. Each distinctive time and movement has its representative spokesmen and prophets. Collections of their books are made and preserved and cherished by their devotees. From the standpoint and date of a given epoch its literature becomes a closed book. Seldom are new authors of importance discovered whose works have to be added to the col-

lections already extant. But in a larger
sense and in the longer perspective the
records accumulate throughout the entire
unfolding life of the race. The Scriptures
in this larger sense include the finest products of the spiritual history of mankind in
all ages. They are the records of the moral
and religious aspirations and ideals of all
humanity. The later stages of this development are not without their influence
upon the Scriptures of past ages. Those
Scriptures of the past are, in a very true
sense, being constantly reinterpreted and
refashioned, while the new material vastly
extends and enlarges the entire body of
literature. Having seen something of the
gradual formation of the canon of our
accepted biblical writings and of the process by which it became set off and apothe-
osized, we may also note the way in which
it is reinterpreted and made continuous
with the ampler Scriptures of the whole
spiritual development of mankind.

The Bible, like other vital books, grows
by constant reinterpretation. This may

be realized through the experience of anyone to whom it is a book of real religious
value. As one makes the Bible his own by
finding in it the passages which appeal to
him and suit his need, he tends to magnify
those selections and ignore the rest. Many
pious souls have for their actual working
Bible scarcely more than the Twenty-third
Psalm, the Sermon on the Mount, the four-
teenth chapter of John, the thirteenth
chapter of First Corinthians, and the last
chapters of Revelation. If you judge by
the interest he displayed in the various
books, the real Bible of Martin Luther con-
sisted of the Epistles of Paul, especially
Galatians and Romans, with the Psalms
and Genesis. He called the Psalms a
"short Bible" and Genesis almost the
noblest book of the Old Testament.
Luther illustrates, too, the fact that the
Bible not only is different for different
people but is different for the same person
at various times in life. At first he rejected the Revelation of John entirely, but
later in life it appealed to him more, though

never as a book of the first importance.
Luther made the Old Testament an allegorical elaboration of the gospel of Christ,
especially as he found that gospel in the
letters of Paul. He saw the mysteries of
the Trinity in the first verses of the first
chapter of Genesis. Zwingli, another of
the reformers, unlike Luther, preached the
New Testament rather than the Old, and
did not regard Paul's letters as the purest
gospel. John Calvin, in his turn, made the
Bible a new book to his generation by a
radically different type of interpretation.
It is said that "for the first time in a thousand years he gave a conspicuous example
of non-allegorical exposition." He even
read the poetry as if it were prose. That
may have been because he had been trained
as a lawyer or because he lacked the poetic
temper. He held the stories of Genesis to
be literal history. The serpent spoke like
a human being when Eve was tempted,
lions lay down with lambs in the ark of
Noah. His view of Christianity was essentially imbued with the Old Testament

standards. To him the Psalms afforded
adequate knowledge of salvation and the
Ten Commandments constituted a sufficient rule of life. In the sixteenth century
he adopted the theological doctrines of the
fourth century and manipulated the texts
of Scripture to support them.

We have thus three Bibles, as one might
say. First that of scholasticism, which
obscured the original Scriptures by the
dogmatic theology of the times. Its understanding of the Christian religion rested
upon the teaching of the church fathers,
with no attempt to get back to the original
text. A second Bible was that of many of
the reformers, of whom Luther is typical.
He went back to the words of the text but
he employed a highly allegorical interpretation. Calvin also took the Bible itself
as the basis of his commentaries and used
a thoroughly literal method, but still with
the point of view and the doctrines of the
fourth century. A third Bible is that of
those modern scholars since the seventeenth century who employed an unham-

pered exegesis in which the Bible for the first time was studied in the light of its own history and by means of free, unbiased investigation.

Another means of realizing how different the Scriptures become under the influence of varying presuppositions may be seen in the comparison of the impressions which different Protestant sects cherish. To one, passages concerning foreordination and election become the standards and controlling determinants; to another, the texts which emphasize the freedom of the gospel; to another, the pivotal texts are those dealing with the second coming of Christ; to another, the miracles of healing are in the foreground. Some magnify withdrawal from the world, renouncing all relations with it so far as possible. A few exalt the evangelization of the world, while some center everything upon a form or a type of organization. From the use made of it the Bible appears in one group to be supremely a volume concerned with future reward and punishment, while to others it is made to be primarily a treasury of mystical visions and forecasts of history. Thus, in a sense, each sect has its own Bible, made by unconscious emphasis upon its favorite interests.

An explanation is suggested by this fact for the growth of the Bible in keeping with the spirit of the age. Gradually the sacred writings have been felt to support causes of reform and progress, abolition of slavery, woman's freedom, economic justice, and prohibition, though in the course of attaining such reforms the Bible has also been appealed to for the sanction of the direct opposites. The realization of this possibility of taking the Bible for the support of widely different points of view has in recent years led to questioning whether there is not some standard afforded by the Bible itself and by the course of history which might furnish a more stable and convincing interpretation. Partly through the interest of our time in social problems and partly through a reading of the whole of Scripture in the light of its greatest messages a better point of view and method have been discovered. The biblical student today seeks to free himself from the presuppositions of the traditional creeds and from the bias of any particular sects. He is better able to do this because the creeds and doctrines have been so thoroughly criticized and appraised in the light of the historical and social conditions out of which they arose. The method of modern scientific analysis and comparison has done its work in this field as elsewhere, and the result is the understanding of the Bible in the light of its own unfolding moral and spiritual conceptions.

The Bible thus attained makes a new and profound appeal to our time, for it is now a collection of writings reflecting the history of a religiously gifted people in their growth and aspirations. Within that history the prophetic utterances of the Old Testament and the words of Jesus mark the high peaks from which all the rest is surveyed and estimated. So aptly and searchingly do the social judgments of the

prophets appeal to the social conscience of
the present that in certain respects they
seem like reformers of the twentieth century.   At the same time the more adequate
knowledge of Jesus has put him above all
the prophets and given him a new hold
upon the spiritual imagination and idealism of the best minds of the new social
order.   In this reconstruction of the biblical material and perspective the book has
become a source of increasing inspiration
and moral incentive.   Some attempts have
been made to reprint the text in a way to
bring out this organization of it around the
character and work of Jesus.   His sayings
have been underlined in some editions.
Some have advocated the re-editing of the
Bible in still more radical ways to make
clear the central, controlling position of
Christ.   It is widely felt that the elimina-
tion of much comparatively irrelevant and
incongruous material would greatly clarify
and magnify the real message of the book
and the cause of true religion.   Out of its
living Word, as from a fountain of cleansed

and purified water, would flow more refreshing streams. This Word, like all
great utterances, is a constant source of
new inspiration and wisdom. It is a growing and inexhaustible treasury of riches and
power for the noblest enterprises of man.

There is a third sense in which the Bible
is a growing collection of sacredly important writings. Not only has it gradually
grown through a long past into the form
in which it was fixed by the Authorized
Version of King James, and not only does
it grow in its use by being interpreted by its
own highest ideals, but it grows in a third
manner. It expands by the assimilation
to itself of the great religious literature
of other peoples and by the contribu-
tions of new prophets and teachers in the
expanding life of the church. The days of
the old exclusiveness in religion as in all
other forms of life are happily passing.
Within a century the sacred books of many
races have become available through the
prodigious labors of armies of scholars.
What Max Mueller did by the translation

of the sacred books of the East is typical and expressive of the new and larger spiritual inheritance we are receiving. Just as a touchstone for understanding Hebrew and Christian documents has been provided in the enlightened social and moral judgment of modern Christendom, so also a standard has been therein secured for appreciation of the best in the great literatures of the world. God has not left himself without a witness among any people. It has come to be regarded as an immoral conception of the divine nature to attribute to him the kind of favoritism which has dominated the church in the past. Everywhere in the prayers and songs and symbolism of the Hindu, Persian, and Confucianist writings are sentiments akin to those of our Old Testament Psalms and Prophets. When the magnet of Christian idealism is brought into contact with them, many great words rise out of these deposits and cling to it with the force of an elemental kinship. Deep calleth unto deep in all the vast waters of man's inner life. Nothing but an arbitrary limitation of the canons of the various faiths prevents the recognition of this fact. As those limitations are swept away in the fires of criticism and of kindling human brotherhood, the common elements are seen and fused together. As internationalism grows and better acquaintance is established, this common possession will become clearer and the mutual understandings come into focus.

Thus the Bible grows by the inclusion of kindred works. The principle of inclusiveness is extending also to contemporary authors. This is strikingly illustrated in the development of the hymnology of the church. It was at first limited to the Psalms. Gradually there grew up beside them the lyrics of the living faith. Sometimes these were the cries of priest or monk or lonely pilgrim. Sometimes they were the music of unordained hearts flowing forth spontaneously. From all such sources the church has appropriated its hymns and carols, its anthems and oratorios. Modern hymnbooks are the blending in Christian

worship of harmonious notes from very
diverse minds and lives. Yet they are not
thereby weakened, but made ampler and
more vital. The songs of David are bound
up with those of the Crusaders and Puri-
tans and modern liberals. Isaac Watts
and Charles Wesley keep company in the
great choir with Bernard of Clairvaux,
Cardinal Newman, and Bishop Brooks.
And what shall be said of the presence
here in an evangelical hymnal of Gilbert
K. Chesterton, Algernon C. Swinburne,
Goethe, Kipling, Oliver Wendell Holmes,
Felix Adler, Tennyson, and Whittier?

In all essential respects the hymnbook is
the expanded edition of the Book of Psalms,
developed and adapted to the enlarging
vision and spiritual aspiration of the
church. Fortunately no censorship nor
creedal test has been able to deprive us of
this rich commingling of the praises and
prayers of men of widely varying outlook.
They have found their place in the sanc-
tuary because of their faith in brotherhood
and unselfish service. Their words have

already become integral parts of our working Bible. They are admitted to the canon of our lyrical Scriptures and they bear appealing witness to the genuine catholicity of our moods of devotion.

It is a simple question which this fact occasions. If the poems of these writers are thus freely incorporated in our Bible, why may we not also add their other equally great and spiritual writings? Have not Tennyson and Whittier and Bryant and Lowell and Phillips Brooks given us other divine gifts of wisdom and beauty? Having opened the way to this great company of prophets and teachers, how shall we again close the doors upon them and exclude them from the sacred canon? And when they have entered not only singing their songs but bringing also their prose and proverbs, how is it possible to separate from them playwrights like Shakespeare and Maeterlinck, or scientists like Kepler and Darwin, or philosophers like John Locke and William James? We cannot believe that God has withdrawn from his

world or is less present than of old. His
living Word finds voice now as in every age.
The divine volume enlarges with the coming of each new prophet. Inspired writers
gather in growing companies to lift the
light of wisdom and beauty upon the ascending path of man's purer and more
abundant life.

CHAPTER IV

THE NEW ORTHODOXY: ITS CHANGING GOAL

Christianity began, if we may trust the impressions gained from a fair reading of the accounts of Matthew, Mark, and Luke, with a challenge to turn from the hope of an immediate establishment of a visible Kingdom of God on earth to the founding of it as an inner kingdom of life and righteousness. In the teaching of Jesus one feels an urgent appeal on behalf of friendliness and generous kindliness between man and man and between man and God. The pure, intimate affection of lovers is exalted into the model for all men and God. Such a love impels to the forgiveness of repeated offenses and to reconciliation with enemies. It leads a man to lay down his very life for his friend. Full of compassion for others, it begets nobility and restraint for one's self. Nor does Christianity leave one with a mere rule and injunction. It furnishes vital human relations in which these qualities are already dominant. Naturally family affection springs into beauty in all human societies. Jesus made that his starting-point. Father and son, neighbor and friend, husband and wife, brother and brother—these are all bound together by an elemental affection which is also capable of extension to strangers and to the invisible God himself. The early disciples confirmed that faith by clinging to each other and to their Master with a loyalty which was spontaneous and measureless. By the charm of his spirit and the appeal of his hopes they were made as one family, as one company of comrades. As they gathered about him on the shore of the lake or sat with him in an upper room at the close of a meal and talked of their dreams, they felt the bonds of their fellowship powerful enough to encompass the world. It was the fact that Christianity became a living communion as well as a doctrine which enabled it to strike root and to resist all opposition. So vivid and imaginative was that fellowship that it could not be broken by time or death. When Jesus was no longer with them in physical presence, they still clung to him as alive in their hearts. After the generation had passed which knew him face to face, another generation, to which Paul belonged, formed a yet more intimate and persuasive comradeship with him. Paul became the apostle of that religion of love and swept through the cities of the gentile world proclaiming it. Everywhere individuals responded and formed societies or churches in which the dominant personality was Jesus, who had died but who lived in the affection of his followers and in the alluring faith in his kingdom of love.

In the feeling of those churches, as with Jesus himself, this world is in close relation to the abode of God in heaven. To Jesus in his reverence and sense of immediate providence the heavenly Father was very near. In his vivid imagination the future

life and Judgment Day were close at hand.
Such matters were not estimated in terms
of space and time, but in their power over
the heart and will.   His followers caught
the same urgency and lived in a universe
whose physical structure was not known
and which had little meaning for them except in moral and religious terms.   The
heavenly realms were just beyond the
clouds, through which in exalted moments
they seemed to penetrate.   There Christ
dwelt at the right hand of God, keeping
watch above his faithful followers, accessible to them in prayer, and preparing to
come again in dazzling glory.

As persecutions arose and the Second
Coming was delayed, attention centered
more on the future heavenly world.   As
the struggles and sufferings increased for
the church on earth, its saints took comfort in the thought of the other world.
In the course of centuries that simple,
natural feeling became organized into a
theology which magnified that other world
still more and became pessimistic about the

present. The great creations of the Greek mind, especially of Plato and Aristotle, were employed to build out that conception to vast proportions. The impressive scholastic philosophy of the Middle Ages marked its climax. Then the discoveries of modern science as to the dimensions of the earth and the heavens added the immeasurable distances of astronomy and the geological periods of time to the picture of the universe. It was in the last century that the difficulties involved in this view became too acute to be borne. Men could not have the same intimate and vivid feeling for a literal heaven so far away in the future and so entirely incongruous with all the discoveries of science. If Laplace, a scientist of rank, could say, "I have swept the heavens with my telescope and find no God there," it is not surprising that many common people have quickly concluded that science has made short work of the whole fabric of religion merely by showing that it employs inadequate conceptions of nature.

So much of the imagery of Christianity was bound up with that little world of visible spaces and appreciable time that the definition of its goal was naturally set in the same framework. The hope of the early Christians was to be worthy to enter heaven and to live there forever. Their faith scarcely sought to redeem the whole world. Roman civilization and degenerate Greece and barbaric tribes offered too great opposition to the early Christians, lowly and impotent in the things of this world. It is not strange that they concluded that their task was to persuade as many as possible to flee this world and only to exist here as though already citizens of heaven. They could learn to be patient with much injustice. Even slaves could bear their servitude in such a way as to convince their masters of the great superiority of the Christian faith. Some day all their burdens would be lifted and they would find themselves transformed into kings and rulers in a happier sphere. They hardly had the opportunity to know that under fair conditions their religion would furnish them the most satisfying life for this present world as well as for the hereafter. As it was, their faith was often the occasion of their suffering and outward misery. Many influences thus conspired to keep their eyes fixed on the other world as their destination and hope. That expectation for the future continued to dominate the church down to very recent times, and is even being renewed by some heralds of the second coming. But another and more attractive goal has arisen before the modern Christian. It is that of the enrichment and enlargement of human life here and now in the conviction that this makes the most of the present and is also the best possible preparation for any future there may be.

This goal is in spirit much like that which constituted the earliest ideal of Jesus, that is, the social message of his teaching. His kingdom of love and service already had its foundation in the natural affection of friends and neighbors. If the

leaven of that gracious faith could have
spread throughout the world without the
persecutions and obstructions which have
been raised against it, perhaps the other-
world goal of the historic church would not
have developed.   But few will doubt that
it was better to have the dream of a kingdom of love preserved to us in the setting
of a distant future life than to lose faith
in it entirely.   Today, however, conditions
have radically changed.   Christianity is no
longer the religion of slaves and underlings.
It is the religion of the mightiest nations on
earth.   Its representatives possess wealth
and power and preferment.   It is no longer
in the attitude of a suppliant, nor in that of
an outsider and antagonist, but it sits in
the councils of state and of industry and
of science.   Men who at least call themselves Christians are among the leaders in
all these things.

For this reason and for many others the
conception of Christianity as centering
chiefly in another life is rapidly losing its
hold.   That which is coming into favor is

the hope of Christianizing the social order itself, as Professor Rauschenbusch has phrased it. Here is taken into account the natural goodness and forward-moving tendency of human nature, its capacity for improvement, for measureless unselfishness, and for nobility and ideality of character beyond all calculation or present imagination. Many comparisons and contrasts between the old and the new are already familiar to popular thought. To state them in balanced sentences has the value of emphasis, though it is not without the dangers of brevity and exaggeration.

The old was static; the new is dynamic. The one sought perfection; the other seeks improvement. One was given; the other is to be gradually achieved. The first was prescribed; the second is to be progressively discovered. That goal depended on providence miraculously transforming the soul; this modern goal depends upon learning by experience as revealed in the lives of great men in the past and in scientific observation and experiment in the present. Religion then was apart from life, from the state, and from practical affairs; religion now is integral with life in all its forms. In the old days it lacked variety and the richness of individuality; in these days it is specialized and made concrete by the peculiar duties and relations given to each person by virtue of his place in society. The old had a separate unique literature; the new regards all noble literature as its medium. The traditional system had a special priesthood; the present order magnifies the priesthood of all true believers. The old attitude despised and feared the natural order which it called the world; the new loves the natural, especially in its service of social ideals. In the past there has been difficulty in using the fine arts in religion; at present they are means of the most impressive symbolization of the new spiritual values. For a long time Christ has been unreal and remote; at last he is becoming human and natural. God was the infinite veiled Being; he is now drawing near even at the risk of seeming finite. Transcendental mysticism was not difficult for the faith of yesterday; a natural, winsome mysticism throbs in the soul of today. The former ideal of the good man was the saintly soul, serene and at peace, withdrawn from the common struggle; the present ideal is of a man sinewy and full of courage, working in the midst of the human tasks, clear-headed and good-natured, conscious of far horizons, to which also his deeds have reference.

At last, then, religion has come to reckon with the fact that its highest quest is not for a supernatural order but just for natural goodness in largest and fullest measure. Through long centuries it has nourished a deep antagonism to mere morality. Natural goodness, it was felt, needed also a churchly consecration. Religion claimed to possess a peculiar sanctity accessible only through its ministrations. It is yet widely viewed in that light. Professor Coe, who has a right to speak on this

subject both as a psychologist and as a
Christian, says:

> Some among us are confused, timid, and non-
> committal because they do not clearly see how
> being religious is different from simply living a
> good life. Others are waiting for some special,
> phenomenal revelation which shall convey a mes-
> sage not otherwise obtainable. All such persons
> are like the bird and the fish in the poem—
>
>> "Oh, where is the sea?" cried the fish; and
>> "Oh, where is the air?" cried the bird.
>
> Let such men know that the religious experience
> is not something different from living a good life,
> but just living it more abundantly.

The task of religion, then, is not that of cultivating a life apart from natural interests
and practical concerns, but is rather the
pursuit of such normal ideals with religious
faith and enthusiasm. When a person de-
votes himself to any cause with zeal and
fidelity, it is said of him that he makes that
cause his religion or he works at it religiously. This is one of the simplest ways
of understanding religion. It is an ex-
traordinary enthusiasm for a cause. As a

recent writer puts it, "Mere morality is prosaic, cool, exact; religion is imaginative, emotional, exaggerated." He adds, "Any man deserves to be called religious by whom an ideal of life has been so heartily and loyally espoused that it lifts him, in some measure, above the power of temptation to seduce or of ill fortune to depress." Accordingly the highest type of religion today is that which has the finest devotion to the most adequate ideal of life. Many sects display the most intense emotional interest in small or partial programs of living. They are devoted to health, or to socialism, or to rescue work in the slums, or to the millennial dawn, or to individual salvation. It is difficult to secure allegiance to a comprehensive program, which is the very thing needed. This is one reason for a religious organization such as the church. It enables each member to have the sense of participating in a many-sided agency the details of which he may not be able to know individually but which are known and cared for by persons in whose judgment and fidelity he is able to confide. In the support of the institution he is aiding many causes and participating in a fuller life than is possible without such an organization. He is also in turn subjecting himself to the larger relations which a social group makes possible. By means of these he is carried along through the interaction of many social currents into larger problems and stimulated to find their solution. The religious society is like the larger community of which it is a part. It makes it possible for an individual to specialize in his own work and yet share in the common, comprehensive enterprise. Just as plasterers and painters can exist only in a society where there are carpenters, brickmasons, truck-drivers, and accountants, so a man who is occupied with the study of the Greek language needs a society where others specialize in cooking, tailoring, engineering, and other things. If he recognizes this fact and realizes that the other activities are as important as his own, and if he maintains respect and neighborliness toward the persons in those other pursuits, then he is so far religious. If he views his own labor as the only kind worth while, or as of supreme importance, then he is selfish. If he thinks of himself as helping in his sphere to the best of his ability to add to the intelligence and beauty and efficiency of the life of a great social order, he is religious.

The religious goal may thus be seen in the way a man takes himself and his work. It may be said that there is but one substance or material or function in what we call life and that everything depends on the way we use it. Each normal person labors, eats, loves, plays, wonders, suffers, and hopes. Whether he is a villain or a saint is determined by the attitude in which he does these things. To be a Christian is to do them generously, with sympathy and intelligence for the ideal human value involved. This may be illustrated in connection with simple acts, such as building a fire in a grate, running a business, or experiencing a friendship. To build a fire for warmth on a cold day might be called a practical act. To do so when the house is already warm in order to enjoy the crackling flames might illustrate the aesthetic interest. To kindle the fire to test the chimney or to make experiments with fuel is the scientific way of doing things. To make the fire for a sick child and to feel in doing so sympathy and human interest for the child and the home and the outreaching significance of its life is to give the act of building the fire a religious quality. A business undertaking, such as conducting a store, may likewise be carried on in a variety of ways. The outward acts may be practically the same. At least to conduct a store it is necessary to purchase goods, to display them, to deal with customers, to employ labor, and to pay taxes. If a man simply says, "Business is business," and works primarily to develop the largest trade possible and to clear the most profits, then we call him practical. Obviously it is not far from that attitude to one of hardness and selfishness and immorality. On the other hand, the merchant may realize that the public is best served by a store which looks out for fair profits, thereby being able to carry a larger stock and to meet the exigencies of trade in the most facile and accommodating manner. In so far as all transactions are open and fair, the community well served, and the labor properly dealt with, the store is a moral institution. But the merchant may take particular pride in his building, in his window displays, in the trimness of his delivery wagons, in the general air of refinement and taste throughout his system. In so far he reveals an aesthetic interest. Now it is conceivable that the merchant is also concerned about improving the wages and working conditions of his employees, in co-operating with other merchants in limiting hours of business, in associating with other citizens to improve the streets, the schools, the living conditions of the community. He is willing to regard his business as a factor in the larger interests of his fellow-men and to use some

of his profits to bring lecturers and entertainers to the city. He will use some of
his earnings to educate a worthy boy he
knows and let the boy decide for himself
later what he will do in the world.   At last,
in his moments of deepest reflection, the
merchant acknowledges that what he has
accomplished has been through combinations of events and the wills of other persons in a most complex and far-reaching
manner. His own part has been real
enough and important; but in relation to
the whole system in which he acts he is but
one factor, dependent and bound up with
the whole system of society, its order, communication, good-will, and fidelity. The
forces of nature also enter into his achievements. Trade is related to crops, and
crops to sun and rain and mellow autumn.
If he is a man as well as a merchant, a person as much as an accountant, will he not
here feel some awe and reverence for the
life which encompasses him, without whose
co-operation he is lost and by whose support he gathers all his gains?   This feeling

is for natural human beings a sense of wider personal relations, of an intimate and vital social fellowship, of devout and reverent consciousness of God. When a man is able now and then to survey his business in that perspective and in that mood, he is religious.

Friendship, too, may be practical and aesthetic, and moral and religious. It may perhaps be any one of the others and not be religious, though that is doubtful; but it is certain that it cannot be religious in the truest measure without also being useful and beautiful and noble.

What, then, is the goal of religion? Not escape from the natural relations, nor the repetition of prayers and creeds, nor the cultivation of communion with ideal beings of the past or of celestial realms. Any of these may be necessary at times, but they are only parts of a larger whole, means to a more inclusive end. The goal of religion is the fulfilment of the normal duties and opportunities of life as we experience it, with sympathy and idealism

and passionately unselfish devotion. This
means that we live the life of our race, eating and loving, toiling and playing, learning
and teaching, watching and praying, ad-
venturing and discovering, suffering and
repenting, for our children and our neighbors, for our country and for humanity,
for the whole dear world and God. If we
build churches, they are way stations and
not terminals. If we picture new Jerusa-
lems, it is not to predetermine for all time
the city of our hearts' desire but to visu-
alize our hopes and to take our bearings
while we journey. We are well aware that
Jerusalem must be retaken and rebuilt over
and over again in the wars of God. The
modern spirit glories in the vision of an in-
definitely great future in which through the
same process of growth and renewal by
which we live now we may go on to greater
and nobler attainments.

We are therefore confronted with the
spectacle of life whose goal is not once for
all set up and fixed, but which is put forward and lifted higher as we labor and

aspire. The dream of the present is of a free society whose chief aim shall be to furnish to all its members the greatest possible power of intelligence, and will, and sympathy, and capacity for social co-operation and progress. That requires intelligence and the constant improvement of popular education. It demands a wholesome and stimulating social atmosphere of freest interaction and emulation for the energizing of the will. It means the closest comradeship and the finest sympathetic imagination, such as is now momentarily realized in times of crises, as in the Japanese earthquake and in the revelations of unselfish devotion through the Red Cross in any disaster.

The function of the church is to make that ideal of a free and growing brotherhood of all mankind real to the experience and to the imagination of men. After all this is not so different from that which it has done for the souls of men in the past. Certainly Jesus summoned his followers into a companionship of adventure and faith on behalf of fuller friendship and deeper love. It may be said that the course of thought since the seventeenth century has been the elaboration of the value of a society in which the individual soul could come to its own in a kingdom of good-will. And surely modern social reformers would be satisfied if they could feel that adequate progress were being made in the permeation of the race with the kindliness and idealism of Jesus. That would mean the cultivation of science to understand what love really requires us to do. It would mean better organization of the state to make the ideals effective. It would mean better care of childhood, in whose plastic soul lie all the possibilities of realizing the most wonderful dreams of the sages and prophets yet to be. We cannot ignore the past nor can we be slaves to it. No more can we merely trust everything to the future; we must anticipate it and live in it as well as in the present.

We are more thoroughly convinced than we ever were before that an international society and brotherhood is not only possible but necessary to the onward movement of the life of every individual of us. Whether we are conscious of it or not, the state of men on the other side of the world affects the welfare of every one of us. It has been religion more than trade or diplomacy or literature which has realized this fact and has acted accordingly by sending heralds of brotherhood literally without purse or scrip into the uttermost parts of the earth. By their labors impressive evidences of the widespreading ideal of brotherhood are increasing over the whole earth. The fact that national greed and selfishness are felt to be inimical to the welfare of mankind is due in no small degree to the realization that it violates the sacred hope and faith which are already steadily rising to consciousness among socialists and laborers as well as among philosophers and missionaries.

Man has climbed far from the depth of his savagery and isolation. He will not forfeit the heights he has gained, nor those

beyond, upon which his eager vision opens.
He has heard the Christmas bells of the
spirit, and he wakes to answer them with
passionate and boundless good-will.

Hark! the bells ringing!
In the deep night, in the depth of the winter of
Man,
Lo! once more the son is born.

O age-long, not in Nazareth alone,
Nor now today—but through all ages of the
past,
The bells of Christmas ringing:
The Savior-music like a dream from heaven
Touching the slumbering heart.

Sweet promise which the people with unerring
instinct cling to!
O winter sun arising never more to set!
O Nature slowly changing, slow transforming
to the hearts of men,
Shrine of the soul, shrine of the new-born god—
of Man himself.

CHAPTER V

THE NEW ORTHODOXY: ITS
NEW DRAMA

If the significance of particular features of the religious life is to be appreciated, they need to be seen and felt in relation to the total living process in which they appear. Any religion remote from one's own is likely to seem to consist of disconnected factors without life or meaning. On this account primitive religions have appeared as the most grotesque and senseless mummery. Interpreters generally fail to perceive the practical ends and intense hopes which dominate the ceremonials even of the lowest savages and the most alien pagans. They see only the weird costumes, the painted bodies, the blood and ochre markings on the ground, the simple sticks and stones, the smoldering fire; they hear through the darkness the moaning, shrieking, and chanting, the fearful noise of the bull-roarers, and at intervals the recital of fanciful myths and strange prayers. Readers often turn away from the accounts of the Indian snake dances or of the Australian initiation ceremonies with disgust and pity. They do not realize what these things really mean to the participants. The snakes are the rain gods, and the gifts of nature depend upon them. The Australians are infusing into the new generation the literal blood and substance of their ancestors. They are reverently endeavoring to guarantee for the future the maintenance of the best things gained in the past. They feel themselves to be *en rapport* with the brave, wise men of the elder days and with the gods who rule the world. They are not engaged in make-believe, but are sharing in the life-and-death struggle to insure the welfare and power of the tribe. Every costume and decoration, every stick and weapon employed, every cry and chant, has a vital place and part in the momentous undertaking.

In principle it is the same with modern religion. Its parts have to be seen fused in the warm, living action of a great enterprise in order to be understood. The costume of a priest, like the uniform of a soldier, implies many things, and, most of all, a profound and tragic cause in which he is engaged. That cause is reflected also in the attitudes characteristic of all religious persons. Their reverence and love and faith are all bound up with the goal they are striving to attain. The same is true of the Bible. It can be appreciated only in reference to the action and movement of the events out of which its words have come. It gives fragmentary and imperfect pictures of the hopes and longings of a people in their struggle to realize their national and cultural ideals. Those ideals were symbolized for them in the majestic figure of their God, moving before them as a pillar of cloud by day and a pillar of fire by night. Riding upon the thundercloud, flashing in the lightnings, and sending his voice pealing among the mountain tops, he was the embodiment of the energy and power with which they felt themselves impelled forward in conquest and in moral aspiration. God cannot be understood apart from his people, with whose will and purpose he is one. Neither can a people be understood without reference to their God. The God of any people may be seen in their purpose, direction, and moral idealism. Without a people God becomes vague, weak, easily disbelieved, and doubted. God cannot be known outside of history and living experience. All attempts to discover him as a fact among the facts of nature have failed. No abstract arguments can demonstrate his being; but wherever you plunge into the red stream of history and enter the pulsing life of actual human beings bound together in great societies, there you find the name and will and power of God.

It is the drama of the religious life, then, which furnishes the explanation of all the factors which appear in it—its attitudes, its dramatis personae, its growing Bible,

and its changing goal. But this drama is
not a stage play. It is not an afternoon's
entertainment. It is not the second-
hand re-enactment of a tragedy which has
been once accomplished. It is the living
action of real life in the natural setting of
land and sea, streets and firesides, shops
and battlefields. It is a drama in which
there are no professional actors, but where
every man takes his rôle in the action by
virtue of his nature and his relation to his
fellows. There is no sharp line between
the audience and the performers. Rather,
in the ceaseless movement of events, individuals arise in their places and perform
their tasks. Some eyes are fixed upon
them where they stand. At the same time
other persons are elsewhere focusing attention. Even the dead do not withdraw
from the drama. Sometimes they continue to arrest the hurrying multitudes
more than do any living kings or warriors.
Their voices seem to grow clearer, their
summons more urgent, as the perspective
in which they appear lengthens.

Each person is thus both actor and observer. The range of his action is far larger than the field of his vision. Many times in his life he is called upon, not to speak lines which he has learned for the occasion, but to improvise actions and words suited to situations which have never existed before in all the world. Upon his decision turns the fate of the whole act and, it may be, of the entire drama. Such momentous events in your personal life were those in which you determined to enter your profession, or to move to this city, or to this neighborhood, or to vote the democratic ticket, or to join the church. Of the same kind, but vaster in results, were the signing of the Magna Charta to guarantee the liberties of England, the Declaration of Independence by the American colonies, the Emancipation Proclamation by Abraham Lincoln, and the Treaty of Versailles which brought to a close the most colossal and the most futile war of history. These were crucial points in the life of mankind. They were of the original,

elemental action which constitutes the
fundamental and essential drama of human
life. These scenes are enacted over and
over again by the play-actors, and something of the original force and meaning is
felt each time. Indeed, the make-believe
drama has its right to exist and its value for
us in the degree to which it is able to re-
instate for all who behold it the sense of a
mighty crisis to be resolved by the deeds
of the individuals present on the stage.
For the time being the actors become the
historical characters responsible for the
course of events, and the audience enter
into the movement of the play, approving
the hero and manifesting indignation
against his enemies. The drama of the
theater has in this way a vital relation
to the actual drama of daily life. When
the spectators have witnessed a stirring
representation of the battles of Washing-
ton's army in our war for independence, they gain new appreciation of what
we owe to those hardy colonists and their
valiant leader.

The drama of the religious life is of the original, elemental kind. Only when it has lost touch with reality does it take on the manner of a spectacle. So long as it is the direct and spontaneous expression of deep needs and true satisfaction its ceremonials are integral parts of life and are just as essential as the most practical activities. That was true of the elaborate ceremonials of the church in the Middle Ages. They were the very means of life to the souls of men. They were not external or artificial or in need of defense. By the elaborate celebration of the Mass men literally obliterated their sins and received in the Eucharist the actual body of God. In that miracle of grace was constantly enacted the drama of the divine love. Every feature of the worship was eloquent with that one fact. The cathedral itself was the architectural expression of the surpassing grandeur of the supersensible world. Its vast arches and high-flung spires towered over man's little form with the distances and glory of that other realm which they symbolized. Whoever has stood in the cathedral at Milan or in St. Peter's at Rome cannot efface the memory of the impression of vastness and magnificence, as if all the devices of wonderful art had been employed to teach man his littleness and transiency in comparison with the infinite and eternal things above him. All other features of the ritual were in keeping with this—the paintings of clouds and cherubim in the lofty ceilings, the sculptured forms of the transfigured saints, high up on the capitals of the giant pillars, the echoing tones of the organ and the ethereal voices of boy choirs, the slowly intoned prayers in an archaic tongue, and the bent, suppliant posture of the worshipers. They were passive and dependent recipients of favors from the world above. They were in search of nothing which they could merit, nor of anything they could create for themselves. None but divine power and infinite condescension could reach their need and lift them up. But so long as all believed in that power and that measureless grace of God bestowed upon man through those channels such rituals and ceremonials were of the very essence of reality. Only with the rise of different conceptions of human nature have these rituals begun to appear as the survivals of a passing world.

Since man has learned to assert himself he has found himself stronger and stronger. He is no longer a passive suppliant, helpless in a predetermined universe. Instead of accepting pestilence and misfortune as the visitations of an all-wise God who sent them for man's discipline, he has set about the task of making such things impossible. The natural causes of many diseases have been found, and those plagues have been eradicated. Encouraged by past success, new and vaster enterprises are under way to gain control of larger and more important areas of life through natural science. Therefore the older drama of religion has become a beautiful work of the past. For the modern man, standing erect in his pride of power, the old ceremonial full of pas-

sivity and surrender is the symbol of a
dying age. He may contemplate it with
a certain admiration and reverence, but he
cannot believe in it nor endeavor to revive
it. It has become a drama in the sense of
being something consciously copied in
order that, through the momentary illusion of its reality, it may be entered into
for appreciation and for the purpose of
knowing more adequately what we have
left behind. Like all things from which
the life has fled, that older drama is no
longer warm and vibrant. Its constituents
have fallen apart. One sees fragments of
its architecture in secular buildings, its
painting and sculpture exhibited in public
displays, its doctrines unbelievable, and its
authority vanished.

Nowhere is the change more apparent
than in the feeling men have about the very
act and attitude of worship. The idea of
worship as mere praise and adulation of
the Creator has become almost irreverent.
God has come to be regarded in so imma-
nent and dynamic a way that it seems

quite inconsistent to conceive him as
honored and gratified by adoration and
flattery, such as were formerly given to
tyrants and despots. Perhaps here is to
be found the source of much indifference
to the churches. Men have given up the
forms and words of worship in their inter-
course with each other and even with their
superiors. In our democracies men do not
bow themselves to the ground nor pros-
trate themselves even before the mightiest
individuals. With open eyes and confident
minds they contend together, seek to co-
operate, and strive to be guided by experience and not by authority. They do not
care for a drama on Sunday which is too
completely contrasted with the drama in
which they live all the week. What they
do crave is some powerful means of discovering the fuller meaning and larger
possibilities of their common life.

The old drama moved between the crea-
tion of the world and the Day of Judgment.
Its origin lay in the inscrutable counsels of
divine wisdom. All of the figures which

moved upon its stage were the puppets of
the omnipotent Will.   Their acts, from the
first deed of rebellion, which brought sin
and its infinite curse, to their acceptance of
the proffered salvation, were foreordained
and once for all decreed.   Even the Re-
deemer, through whom the bondage was
broken, did not act in his own right but was
sent into the world and given up to bitter
pain and death for man's deliverance.   To
the end of time the efficacy of his atone-
ment was to remain a fathomless mystery,
for not until the grand assize at the great
Day of the Lord could it be known who are
worthy of blessing and who deserve the
curse.   The services of religion, under that
conception, have been largely devoted to
cultivating a sense of humility and of un-
worthiness in the worshiper and an attitude of resignation for any fate which may
befall!

The new drama starts with man's life on
the earth and with the upward and forward
tendency within it.   It shows, from the
earliest records, efforts toward something

better and loftier.   Everywhere are temples
and tombs and the sign of uplifted hands.
In and around these have flowed the intense desires and aspirations of the unsatis-
fied soul of man, restless in his age-long
quest.   Often mistaken as to the source of
his success, always burdened with superstitions and misconceptions of himself and
his world, nevertheless he has continued to
follow the gleam.   At last he is finding out
the immediate causes of many of his bless-
ings and his ills.   With a new joy and courage in his discovery of scientific knowledge
and power he is preparing for still greater
mastery and progress.   With all of his old
reverence for life and with greater zest he
is not merely *seeking* a city which hath
foundations.   He is building it.   He does
not just sit silently listening in his worship,
but he wrestles with God and, like Jacob of
old, exacts his blessing.   The drama which
he is enacting is one of intense activity and
profound thoughtfulness.   This has quite
changed the meaning of worship.   It is
now no longer the contemplation of a series

of celestial events in which man beholds himself the passive recipient of divine favor or wrath. It is rather the survey of the long path of past experience and the memory of the heroic actors who have toiled there and the anticipation of the further extension of that path by labor, intelligence, and unselfish devotion. Through it all run the realization of the magnitude of the forces involved, the incalculably great scale of the events transpiring, and the tragic character of the smallest word and deed. It is this richness and inexhaustible nature of experience which constitutes its divine quality. But the divine is no more separate and aloof. It is within and organic with the human. We surrender the old contrast of the human and the divine, not by eliminating either one to retain the other, but by insisting that life as we find it has in it the warmth and intimacy of the human and also the dynamic and the outreach of the divine. Life is in this respect all of a piece, varied and intricate, but undivided.

In the drama of the religious life as thus conceived the congregation is the unit of action and expression. Not the public service, so largely the function of the minister and the choir, but the less formal meetings of the church for counsel and conference illustrate it best. The local church is a kind of epitome of the whole social order. It undertakes to guide itself by the spirit and ideals of a truly religious society. It can succeed only as all of its members consciously and enthusiastically enter into that endeavor. Three things are continually dramatized in every church, no matter how imperfectly: the vast implications of our life, the intimate personal feeling of being at home, and the alluring hope of a better future.

The greatness of man's life in the old drama was set forth in the very fact of the condescension of heaven to take note of him.   In the new he is accorded a real part. A mother feels herself intrusted with a wonderful share in the life of the world through her child.   She is constantly hoping to nourish and train him so that he may bless mankind. She cannot hide from herself the question of his future usefulness. If he could measure up to her wishes for him he would bring some good invention, make some discovery, accomplish some distinguished service. In caring for him she thinks of herself as performing a task for thousands who are to be helped by him. As she herself is the inheritor of the affection and yearning watchfulness of countless ancestors, so in turn she is to transmit the stream of life through him to countless other human beings. Religion calls attention to these great distances and to these wonderful implications in the plot of every human life. Even a sparrow is upheld by the whole power of the universe, and man is of more value than many sparrows. He is therefore called upon to live, not for the passing hour, but for all that relates to it and for all that grows out of it. In this consists man's true nobility: He views himself more truly as the child of the ages than as the grass of the field. We are gaining more adequate means of estimating human influence and responsibility. Ibsen's *Ghosts* is an artistic expression of this fact. The great tables of the statistics of heredity tell the same story. It was recognized by George Eliot as "the sweet presence of a good diffused, and in diffusion ever more intense!"

The religious representation of life also emphasizes the sense of being at home in the world and of extending a yearning love to all individuals. The good shepherd goes in search of the one lost sheep. The redemptive sympathy of modern society reaches out toward the poor, the lonely, and the separated souls. Religion might well dramatize the work of social settlements, of public schools, of boards of health and morals. The necessity of co-operation has never been brought home to men in the history of the world before as at the present time. Society insists upon closer supervision of private affairs, of individual property, and of business. In levying and paying taxes, in the intelligent promotion of social feeling, a **degree** of voluntary consolidation and unification has been attained of which earlier centuries only dreamed.

No man liveth unto himself now. That has suddenly come to be far more than a statement of pious sentiment. It is felt to be the very condition and necessity of any kind of existence. This dependence of the individual upon his group and his participation in its practical and ideal life is one of the deepest and most vital facts of the religious life. The church has need to extend this principle in more vivid and commanding ways to individuals not included at present in the immediate circle of the church. It becomes true of the great souls of the past too. They also co-operate with us. By their writings and their deeds they participate in our deliberation and in our estimate of the value and sanctity of our religious ideals. They suffer and toil with us, and their words of courage and comfort are like counsels of our dearest friends.

Not only does the church seek to keep
alive in its members the sense of the dignity
of human life and of personal worth, but it
also dramatizes the hopes which are cherished and toward whose fulfilment every
energy is dedicated. These hopes revive
in the company of those who seek them and
contemplate them. In the older hymns
the sentiment was, "I'm but a stranger
here; heaven is my home." In the newer
hymns we sing, "We are builders of that
city."

Religious souls have been variously represented in art as in life. They have been
shown as solitary pilgrims in their search
for God and peace of soul. They have
been portrayed as "a noble army, men and
boys, the matron and the maid, who
climbed the steep ascent of heaven, thro'
peril, toil and pain." But there is something still more appealing in the dream of
them as builders of a beautiful city.

The city is becoming more impressive as
a symbol of the enlarging spiritual life
of man. It affords opportunity for com-

panionship, for intelligent concerted action, for effective brotherhood, and for means for growth.   Man can see in the city the fruits of his labors and the consequences of his mistakes.   He is thereby brought to terms with his own conduct and furnished incentives for indefinite improvement.   No longer solitary or ascetic, militant or visionary, the Christian sees rising about him "the glorious golden city."   In the words of Felix Adler's beautiful hymn:

> We are builders of that city;
>   All our joys and all our groans
> Help to rear its shining ramparts;
>   All our lives are building-stones:
> Whether humble or exalted,
>   All are called to task divine;
> All must aid alike to carry
>   Forward our sublime design.
>
> And the work that we have builded
>   Oft with bleeding hands and tears,
> And in error and in anguish,
>   Will not perish with our years:
> It will last and shine transfigured
>   In the final reign of Right;
> It will merge into the splendors
>   Of the City of the Light.